Praise for *String of Pearls*

Reading Diane Bailey's book, *String of Pearls*, is like sitting down and having a heart-to-heart honest conversation with the author. She talks candidly about her life, the pain of a bad first marriage and divorce, and her thoughts about suicide. Throughout her well-written and tender book, Bailey focuses on God's Word, how God brought her through painful experiences, and what she learned from Scripture.

I highly recommend Diane Bailey's book, *String of Pearls*. It tells a story everyone should read, and gives meaningful Scriptural advice throughout its pages.

—Denise George
Author: *Johnny Cornflakes:
A Story About Loving the Unloved*
www.authordenisegeorge.com

In my friend, Diane's, new book, *String of Pearls*, she uses her homespun wit, wisdom, bare-knuckles approach to life to transport us from our isolated "own little world" to a deep sense of connectedness to our roots. Not only does Diane help us to learn from our mother Eve, but also to receive our ultimate healing and value in the Father of us all. Well done, Diane!

—Kimberly L. Smith
Author: *Passport through Darkness*
President of Make Way Partners

Praise for String of Pearls

In *String of Pearls*, Diane Bailey writes from the heart as she struggles with being a young wife and mother. Readers will relate to ordinary problems common to all women—from the journey of Eve through the pages of time.

Like the threads of a tapestry, Bailey weaves her experiences and connects them with Scripture to help the reader understand that negative consequences can be used to God's greater good.

—**Carolyn Tomlin**
co-Author, *The Secret Holocaust Diaries:
The Untold Story of Nonna Bannister*

String of Pearls

String of Pearls

Diane Woodman Bailey

BorderStone Press, LLC

2011

First Edition

String of Pearls

Author: Diane Woodman Bailey
Editor: Gail Waller

Published by BorderStone Press, LLC, PO Box 1383, Mountain Home, AR 72654
Dallas, TX /Memphis, TN

www.borderstonepress.com

© 2011 by BorderStone Press, LLC

Copy editor: Dr. Roger D. Duke
Supervising editor: Brian Mooney

All rights reserved. With the exception of short excerpts for critical reviews, no part of this publication may be reproduced, stored in a retrieval system, or transmitted in any form by any means, electronic, mechanical, photocopy, recording, or otherwise, without prior permission of the publisher, except as provided by USA copyright law.

Reasonable efforts have been made to determine copyright holders of excerpted materials and to secure permissions as needed. If any copyrighted materials have been inadvertently used in this work without proper credit being given in one form or another, please notify BorderStone Press, LLC in writing so that future printings of this work may be corrected accordingly. Thank you.

Permission granted to use quoted material from: *Prayer Portions*, © by Sylvia Gunter, The Father's Business, P. O. Box 380333, Birmingham, AL 35238, www.thefathersbusiness.com
Email FathersBiz@cs.com

Internet addresses (Web sites, blogs, etc.) and telephone numbers printed in this book are offered as a resource to you. These are not intended in any way to be or imply any endorsement on the part of the editor or BorderStone Press, LLC, nor do we vouch for the content of these sites and numbers for the life of this book.

Unless otherwise indicated, Scripture quotations are taken from the New American Standard Bible®, Copyright © 1960, 1962, 1963, 1968, 1971, 1972, 1973, 1975, 1977, 1995 by The Lockman Foundation. Used by permission.

BorderStone Press, LLC publishes this volume as a document of critical, theological, historical and/or literary significance and does not necessarily endorse or promote all the views or statements made herein, or verify the accuracy of any statements made by the Author. References to persons or incidents herein may have been changed to protect the identity of those involved.

ISBN: 978-1-936670-00-0

Library of Congress Control Number: 2010943477

Interior is acid free and lignin free.
It meets all ANSI standards for archival quality paper.

Table of Contents

Acknowledgements iii

Introduction v

Chapter 1 1

Chapter 2 39

Chapter 3 67

Chapter 4 95

Chapter 5 123

Chapter 6 147

Chapter 7 169

About the Author

Acknowledgements

—To my husband Joseph, Thank you for all the encouragement, patience and challenging conversations that gave me the courage to write this book. I love you.

—To my friends Jeanne and Eloise for all the love and time listening to me talk all of this through. God has given me such great treasures in you.

—To Gail Waller for the hours of editing. I am so thankful for your knowledge and friendship.

—To BorderStone Press, LLC, in particular Dr. Roger Duke and Brian Mooney, for giving me the opportunity to have a lifetime dream fulfilled.

Introduction

Who is a God like Thee,
who pardons iniquity
and passes over the rebellious act
of the remnant of His possession?
He does not retain anger forever
because He delights in unchanging love.

Micah 7:18

HAVE YOU EVER LOOKED BACK AT TIMES in your life and realized the hand of God had been with you; but at the time it seemed all was darkness and sorrow?

Haven't we all?

String of Pearls

I was in a bad marriage when life took a horrible turn for the worst and I found myself a single mother of two pre-teens, a single head of household, with meager finances.

I had rebelled against the warning signs God placed in front of me, endured some bad decisions of others, and found myself in circumstances that many women fear the most: rejection, abandonment, and despair. For a short time the only answer seemed to be ending my life.

The Grace of God is the only way I can explain my survival. Survival that was mental, physical, emotional and spiritual. Looking back I can see the hand of God moving, protecting and creating situations that were good for me, but at the time He was difficult to see.

Introduction

Looking back I wonder about what I learned, which is what this book is about. Before my struggles, when the sign said "Don't," I "Did." Now, when God says, "Don't," I "Don't."

The rules are in place to validate, not negate, my life. If God says, "Don't," then there is a good reason and I don't have to know what He knows. In fact, the older I get and the more I understand what He understands, I would often rather go back to a state of ignorant bliss! But once you cross the line and know something, you can't un-know it.

So what now? I had crossed the city limits line into Don't-Ville and knew the sorrow that lives there. I also knew the relief and joy of my King in Shining Armor rescuing me.

Now what was I to do with what I knew?

String of Pearls

Christ had rescued me from sure death and given me a new life, beginning with Him as the Head of the Household. He turned my sorrow into a life of joy. He took my sorrows and turned them into victory and a testimony of Christ in my life.

As a grain of sand causes pain and sorrow to an oyster, my rebellion had caused pain and sorrow to myself and to God. But just as the pain the oyster experiences causes it to respond in a way that brings forth a pearl, my response to my sorrow drove me to my knees with the ugly, mascara running, snot blowing, and rug-eating repentance that moved the heart of God. His Word says in Psalms 51:17, "The sacrifices of God are a broken spirit; A broken and contrite heart, O God, Thou wilt not despise."

Introduction

When we become broken and contrite over our sins and call out to God, He comes and does what we cannot. He can take our sorrows and change them into a pearl of great value. We can take all of our sorrows to Christ, and by the end of our lives have *A String of Pearls*.

Soli deo Gloria!

Chapter 1

Worrying, *Like Rocking* . . .

*Faith is being sure of what we hope for,
and the assurance of what we cannot see.*

Hebrews 11:1

"I didn't ask to be born!" shouted my teenage daughter from the bedroom. "It's not fair. Nobody else has to do this!"

Good thing you didn't ask to be born today, I thought to myself.

Today the answer would be no, not today.

STRING OF PEARLS

"Well, tell God, because He thought it was a good idea—at the time," I replied toward her bedroom. "And your room still has to be cleaned before you go to Tiffany's house."

I whispered a prayer. "Father, help me to survive this child, and please make sure she gets caught on everything that tries to divide her from you."

When my children were born I had wonderful dreams for them, as any mother who is in love with their babies would! As they grew, I could see gifts and talents that God had generously placed in them, and I began to encourage them to develop those gifts and talents. As they grew older and became increasingly independent, I watched with joy at times, and cringed at other times, as they made choices that would direct the course of their

Worrying, *Like Rocking...*

lives. I loved watching them set healthy goals and go after them, and I was horrified when they made choices that I knew were prerequisites to disaster. Without a doubt these were times, more than any other times in my life, when I grew the most in my prayer life and in knowing God's Word.

"Trust in the Lord with all your heart and lean not on your own understanding." Proverbs 3:5 is a verse I frequently quoted to myself. How could I lean on my own understanding?

When I was growing up I had baby dolls, and an instruction manual came rubber-banded to them. But the more I lived with my own children, these precious earthen vessels, the more I was aware that no instruction manual had been rubber-banded to them. I knew almost immediately that I would need someone bigger and smarter than I was to help parent these children God had given to me. I am so thankful that in His wisdom and mercy He had planned for me to need His help from the very beginning.

God was a parent to Adam and Eve, and He planned for them from the beginning. He provided them with what they needed. He planted the Garden and chose plants that were good for food. He made beautiful flowers for their viewing pleasure. He gave them promises for the future, and it was going to be a long future, you know, because He did not forbid them from eating from the tree of life. Maybe that tree was there in case they needed some kind of life refill, when there was too much to do and not enough day.

Worrying, *Like Rocking...*

Now let us journey with Eve and the progression of woman through the pages of time, from the Garden to the cross and into our own lives. Through this process, we see how Christ hands down consequences, redeems, and uses Eve's bad choice to His greater good.

Before Eve, it was just God and Adam, walking in the Garden together, naming the beasts of the field, and every bird of the sky, and giving instructions, God to man. God's instructions to Adam were to cultivate and keep the Garden. The Garden was Adam's responsibility under God's guidance.

The words in God's instructions to Adam are *abad* (cultivate) and *shamar* (keep). *Abad*, cultivate: it means to work, to labor, to toil, to make weary. Adam had responsibility, but with that responsibility came the satisfaction of working and of being in an intimate relationship with the Lord. I wish so much that we could walk physically in the cool of the day with the Lord. Oh, the questions I would have for him. "And where did You come up with the idea of blue? Was it something that came to You in your sleep? Oh, wait—You don't sleep." "How long did it take You to work out the nervous system?" "And the solar system—do You ever have to give any of that a push, or does it work until You say stop?" These are some of the things I would love to know, to hear how He thought it all up, and I would have loved to help the Lord keep the Garden.

The word for keep is *shamar*. It means to place a hedge, to guard, to watch, to keep safe. It is how a shepherd cares for his flock. Adam was not running around the Garden in his

Worrying, *Like Rocking...*

birthday suit, smelling roses and eating grapes as he is sometimes depicted in children's books. Adam had *shamar* to do.

God created us and knows our every thought. He knows that for us to appreciate the gifts He gives to us, we need instruction and active participation. So He gave both to Adam in the form of responsibility for the Garden. And since the Garden would be an arduous task, God knew that Adam would need a helpmate. But in the entire Garden, there was not yet a suitable mate, so God made one: Eve. He allowed Adam to evaluate and name the animals, and in doing so, Adam discovered the character of the things he was to keep and cultivate. This knowledge let him recognize God's gift of Eve when she appeared.

String of Pearls

Why do you think the Lord made Adam do all that work naming animals, but did not let him find what he was looking for in a mate? Proverbs 25:2 says, "It is the Glory of God to conceal a matter, but the glory of kings is to search out a matter." I believe that God delights in treasure hunts; there are wonderful mysteries to be solved in the discovery of His perfect will.

When God announced that it was not good for Adam to be alone and He would give him a mate, I think that Adam was excited about what was to come, but I don't think what ensued is what Adam expected. Every animal that God created came to Adam. Everything but the promised gift came his way. Can you imagine? "The big grey thing with the long nose . . . elephant . . . no match. The black and white bird with no legs, can't fly . . . penguin . . . no

Worrying, *Like Rocking...*

match. The thing that looks like a combination of duck and beaver . . . platypus . . . (did You use leftover parts on him?) . . . no match.

Matthew Henry suggests, "God gave him all the wrong matches first so when the correct one was in front of him, he would quickly recognize her."[1] And recognize her he did. The first words from his mouth were, "Bone of my bones, flesh of my flesh, This one shall be called Woman, because she was taken from Man." How beautiful! If the love of my life came up and these were his first words to me, I'm not sure if I would laugh or swoon. Either way, he would have my attention.

I find it interesting how the Hebrew words work the same as English words here. In

---

[1] Matthew Henry, *Commentary on the Whole Bible*, Peabody, MA: Hendrickson Publishers, Inc., (2008), 8.

STRING OF PEARLS

Hebrew, woman is *ishshah* and man is *ish*. Just as *man* is the root of *woman*, *ish* is the root of *ishshah*. Is there someone in your family who carries part of your name, or were you named after someone? My middle name, Elizabeth, comes from my Aunt Lib (Elizabeth) who helped to raise my mother after her parents died. It is such an honor for me to carry part of her name. Just as Aunt Lib waited patiently for me to be born to greet her new namesake, man waited patiently for the promised helpmate. And when she arrived he recognized her as an important completion of himself and gave her part of his name.

Waiting patiently for God is not the most fun part of the Christian walk. There are times in all of our lives when we are not sure we have heard God correctly, whether it is because the

Worrying, *Like Rocking...*

answer is hard, or it is frustrating, or we think it is taking too long. Some days we feel like yelling, "I didn't ask to be born into this mess!" But knowing the Word of God is one way we can pace and strengthen ourselves, not running ahead of His plan or giving up when it seems too slow in coming.

This verse comforts me: "For the vision is yet for the appointed time; It hastens toward the goal, and it will not fail. Though it tarries, wait for it; for it will certainly come, it will not delay" (Habakkuk 2:3). Though it tarries, wait for it. Now that is the hard part. Do you ever feel like saying, "God, I need patience in the wait, and I need it now!"

Waiting can be difficult, and if we are not careful, we can give in to wayward thoughts and lofty imagination. We can become so

String of Pearls

focused on the request we have before the Lord that we become obsessed, allowing it to dominate our thoughts. When this happens, our prayer request divides us from God.

We think about our request all day long, daydreaming about how we can make it what it should be. We run for immediate gratification. We get on the phone and talk our problems out with our friends, especially when it comes to those we love. Waiting for God is so difficult; our energy level is high with anxiety. But it is always wise to run to God's throne before running to the phone, and waiting can be a good time for other things. Use some of that energy to memorize scripture, or meditate on the Word of God. Use that energy to accomplish good instead of worrying your way to ulcers.

Worrying, *Like Rocking*...

Allow God to reveal to you the Scriptures that apply to your situation. Applying God's Word to our lives is vital to our survival. Write these Scriptures down in a prayer journal; share them with women of faith who can come alongside you as you wait on the Lord. Memorize Psalm 23, or if you are feeling the challenge, try memorizing Psalm 91. It is sometimes called the "Warrior's Psalm," which comes from a story told about the 91st Brigade during World War I. This unit recited the 91st Psalm daily, and was involved in three of the bloodiest battles of the war. But while other units were counting up to 90% casualties, the 91st Brigade did not suffer a single combat-related death.

As I wait, I also find it helpful to pray for others in the same situation. I go to them and simply ask how I can pray for them, and through this I have seen the situations of other people—situations similar to my own—change when I include them in my prayers. When I include others with similar burdens in my prayers, I am comforted too, as I wait for God's answer. This seems to touch the heart of God. To be burdened by your own sorrow, yet reach out to help others, is a characteristic of Christ that God will not overlook.

Let us consider two things:

1. *Delay is not the same as deny.* 1 Thessalonians 5:21-22: "Examine everything carefully; hold fast to that which is good; abstain from every form of evil." An answer that seems to be delayed does not mean that God is denying our requests; it takes time to evaluate. Sometimes, like with Adam, He allows

Worrying, *Like Rocking...*

us to experience the wrong answer first so that we'll recognize the right one when He sends it our way. We frequently need to examine and discern differences. It can be difficult to recognize the correct answer on the first try, and when we are waiting desperately for God to speak to us, we might grab the first thing that comes along. A little instruction and time can keep us from making a mistake.

2. *Patience gains the promise.* As 2 Peter 3:9 tells us, "The Lord is not slow about his promise as some count slowness, but is patient toward you not wishing for any to perish but for all to come to repentance." When we are hurting, it is difficult to see past our own pain. Perhaps the delay in answers and promises is not about you; perhaps the Lord is bringing others into the fullness of His plan.

String of Pearls

In my experience, instructions usually come from time spent in His Word and in prayer. We can receive instruction many different ways: we may read a verse from the Bible, hear something repeated, have a dream, or a friend may speak directly to our thoughts.

My friend Eloise and I were praying about where the Lord wanted our intercessory prayer group to go in ministry. One day I told her I tripped over, and kept tripping over, a particular book at home and I wondered if God was trying to tell me something. She said that she had a book that kept popping up for her too. Both books, it turned out, were about fasting. When we met again, we brought the books, pulled them out of our purses, and they were the same—*Fasting* by Jentezen Franklin. I believe God had given us our instructions.

Worrying, *Like Rocking...*

Our Lord delights in creation, process, and revelation. He wants us to seek Him and find Him. Deuteronomy 29:29 says, "The secret things belong to the Lord our God, but the things revealed belong to us and to our sons forever, that we may observe all the words of this Law." God's patience in the answers and promises allows us time to share with others what He has revealed to us and to teach His words to others by explaining the hope that is within us. Once we have a piece of the secret things, we teach it to our families. Now what we have been hoping for becomes a generational blessing and an inheritance for the next generation.

Sometimes not knowing the exact answer or timing allows us to explore all areas as we look for Him. In this exploration we inadvertently engage in activities that seem mundane (like naming animals), and as we are faithful to the mundane tasks before us, He will be faithful in bringing us face-to-face with the promises and answers we seek. In addition, what we consider mundane may become a foundation.

When I was a child, my daddy wrestled with us three girls and our baby brother. We would wrestle for what seemed like hours, with my mom in the background warning Daddy to be careful with us. We would try sneak attacks on Daddy, all of us jumping on him at the same time, laughing and playing until one of us would get upset and the game would be over. Little did I know back then that Daddy was teaching us to defend ourselves. One of the lessons I remember to this day is to grab an opponent's head. "Grab the head!" he would

Worrying, *Like Rocking...*

say. "Grab the hair, face, eyes, whatever you can hold on to, because wherever you lead the head, the body will follow."

His words are also true in our thoughts as well as our prayer life. As we wait on the Lord, we must guard our head, our mind; it is the first target of attack. There is an expression, "If you can believe it, you can achieve it." It is common enough, but those words can work for us or against us. Choose carefully what you allow your mind to believe or dwell on. If the enemy has your head, your body will follow.

Satan knows that our weak spot is our family; it is his second area of attack. He comes in with illness, rebellion, financial loss, desire for gain, property damage, failing grades, or any number of things. When we don't see anything changing, even after years of prayer,

STRING OF PEARLS

we can become discouraged and despair. You and I could make a long list. If Satan can control our thoughts, so that we obsess over a problem instead of praising our Lord or encouraging others in the faith, then he has been successful and we have made his job easy. Remember, worrying is like rocking in a rocking chair; it gives you something to do, but it accomplishes nothing.

Instead, Philippians 4:6-9 advises us to "be anxious for nothing, but in everything by prayer and supplication with thanksgiving let your requests be made known to God. And the peace of God, which surpasses all comprehension, shall guard your hearts and your minds in Christ Jesus. Finally, brethren, whatever is true, whatever is honorable, whatever is right, whatever is pure, whatever is

Worrying, *Like Rocking*...

lovely, whatever is of good repute, if there is any excellence and if anything worthy of praise, let your mind dwell on these things."

When waiting on the Lord, guard your mind. Keep it busy on the things that lift your head and glorify God. Psalms 22:3 says, "Yet Thou are holy, O thou who art enthroned up the praises of Israel." The King James Version says that he "inhabitest;" he inhabits the praises. The Hebrew word for this is, *yashab*, meaning to dwell, to sit down, to abide. God's enthronement, his habitation in praise, is your weapon in prayer. Praise Him, for He will abide. He will sit down in your praises.

If you are wrestling in your mind, waiting for God to answer, then praise Him. Think back on all the times you prayed to the Lord Jesus and He answered you, and praise Him for these times. A woman relative of mine did not have the best taste in boyfriends as a teen and very young adult. I and others prayed for years for Jesus to turn her heart to a godly man. I am glad to report that she did break up with her boyfriend and married a godly man who is the answer to our prayers. Let this be encouragement for you. Thank God for those times you can remember Him helping you, knowing that though you cannot see the answers, or His hand working on your current situation, you know He has been there for you before and He will move for you again.

Add James 4:7-8a to your arsenal: "Submit therefore to God. Resist the devil and he will flee from you. Draw near to God and He will draw near to you."

There you have it.

Worrying, *Like Rocking...*

When you are praising, God is near you, and if He is near you, guess who is not? Draw near to God with your praises; rejoice in Him, for He *is* good, and his mercy *is* everlasting. You can do this! As my mom says, "Birds of a feather flock together." You are in the family of God if you have accepted Jesus as your Savior, believe that He died on the Cross for your sins, and that God raised Him from the dead as the first of many. Therefore we should behave as children of God, and staying close to family helps.

Another way I have discovered to combat the pressures of being a woman is praise. Turn up that music, sister! Dance and praise! Praise until you reach the throne of God. Go for a walk, and sing all the worship songs and hymns you know. Go ahead and give the neighbors something to talk about, or perhaps something to ask you about. Like, "What have you got to be so joyful about?"

If you have not accepted Christ as the Lord of your life and your Savior, let me invite you to do so right now. The words are simple, and He will give you the faith as well as the understanding as you see Him. "Lord Jesus, I know I cannot save myself. As hard as I try, it still isn't good enough. I believe that You died for my sins and were raised from the grave. Please forgive my sins on the basis of what You did on the cross for me, and teach me to live as You lived. Teach me of You. Come into my heart and live in me, directing me in the way that You know is best for me. In Your name I pray. Amen."

Worrying, *Like Rocking*...

I hope you will call someone about your decision. Find a church that teaches the Word of God, and allow the women of that church to gather you into your new family, the family of God.

I love older women and frequently go to them for advice. Once you find an older woman in your church who has the joy of the Lord and wisdom from above, invite her to have coffee or lunch with you. These women are founts of priceless information and love. I am very blessed to have three older women in my life. One is my mother, who led me to Christ at a young age and continues to encourage me to bring all things to Him. Another precious woman is Sara, who gave me wonderful, godly counsel as I was mourning the obvious death of my marriage. She encouraged me to face each situation in such a way that I would have no regrets. And I went to my friend Jane when I wasn't sure about someone who was marrying into my family. The first thing out of her mouth was, "Well, Diane, you are going to remember first of all that you are a Christian and show him the love of Christ, whether you like him or not," and eventually I came to love this new member of our family.

I have needed all these women at some point in my life. I think of Eve and bet Eve would have liked an older woman to talk with, someone who had been down that road before her and could give her good advice.

Women were created to be helpmates. Caring for someone brings great satisfaction. Encouraging someone to be their best, to step into all that Christ has created him or her to be,

Worrying, *Like Rocking*...

is rewarding. If you are not married, you may be a helpmate of sorts to your employer. Perhaps there is an elderly person who needs assistance, or an orphanage in your area that needs help. Maybe you have time to partner with a crisis center in need of volunteers. If you don't have children, there are women around you who need encouragement, the kind that comes only from Christ. Reach out to them; you may be the only example of Jesus they ever see.

Women are hard workers, wearing many hats during the day. Joseph might have had a coat of many colors, but it was nothing compared to the hats that women wear! We have a purple hat with a geranium in it to put a smile on other people's faces. We wear a fireman's hat to put out the fiery argument

String of Pearls

between siblings, a nurse's hat to give hugs and Band Aids when one of the children's bike tricks did not go so well, and those are just the family hats. We wear lots of hats for work and for volunteering, maybe as a baseball mom or a civic group leader.

We do so much that we can become tattered and worn, but that is not God's perfect will for us. Do not allow the stress of being a woman to take hold of you. Thinking we need to take on so much is a lie from the pit. It tells us that we must produce to prove our worth.

Boloney!

There *are* seasons of doing more than we think is possible—think about new mothers, or new mothers with twins, or single mothers with teens, or working mothers with children to raise. And then there are mothers who do all of

Worrying, *Like Rocking...*

it and care for a parent or struggle in a troubled marriage. In seasons like these, we find a side of Christ that we would never know any other way. But there should be seasons of rest and comfort as well. Ask the Lord about your life; then write down your impressions of what He is telling you. He will speak to you; He longs for quiet time alone with you. He is the best Father, and He wants the best for you.

As you abide in Him, His peace that passes all understanding will become a robe of authority to walk in. His joy will take over and become a crown on your head. You will have the authority of Christ to press in on the wrongs of this world in prayer. Allow the Holy Spirit to show you your authority in Christ and also to show you areas to let go. Always remember that it is not you, but He who works through you. Draw near to God as you wait for your answers, knowing He hears and is actively working for you because you love Him and are called according to His purpose.

And stop thinking only about your struggles. Pray for others. If there is a burden on your heart, maybe God has put it there. Does your heart cry out for our soldiers, natural disaster victims, problems in the church, or widows and orphans, our cities or country? James 1:27, "This is pure and undefiled religion in the sight of our God and Father, to visit orphans and widows in their distress, and to keep oneself unstained by the world." Do not dismiss these cries of the heart. God may be allowing them to be placed in front of you because He wants us to interact in prayer. What if He is giving you the gift of being an

Worrying, *Like Rocking*...

intercessor or prayer warrior? Imagine such an honor.

This is an area He called me into. I fought it for so long. "I have enough to deal with, God. I don't want to deal with other people's stuff!" My "no" had little effect on His plan for my life.

I now am a part of a prayer group at our church. We have a list of prayer requests that is kept private. There are times I intercede for others as the Lord brings people and situations to my mind as well.

Now that I have answered "yes" to the call of praying for others, God has done the most amazing things with prayer. There was a time that I woke in the night. I had a picture in my mind of a woman I had never met laying facedown in snow. I began to pray for her survival. I didn't know what else to pray about.

String of Pearls

I questioned God about whether or not I was making up this scenario. The next day the news reported that that morning a woman who had been lost for many days in the mountains had been found. My jaw just about hit the floor!

Has He ever done that with you? Have you even had an impression about something but you really did not know if it were really God? Go ahead and begin to intercede. You may never know until you get to heaven if it were true. Then you may meet that person in heaven, face to face. How cool is that?

I have learned that if I feel critical about someone or a situation, then I am probably being called to pray for it. For so long I used my discernment for gossip. Even if I did not know the person, I might call a friend and tell her

Worrying, *Like Rocking*...

about the tacky outfit someone was wearing at the grocery store. Lord, forgive me.

Or maybe you know someone who is obsessed with her children, allowing them to control her life. Be kind instead of critical. There is either a disorder or a root of fear., but either way she needs your prayers. There is always a reason for the weird things people do, and we all have weird things in our lives! Don't deny it, you know it is true. Like why Uncle Albert insists on wearing white knee socks with black shoes and shorts, why Mom leaves her coffee in the microwave everyday and wonders why she can't find it. It can be small and humorous or big and debilitating. But we all have stuff that is a little strange about us where we could be the topic of someone else's conversation. Let us all try to show a little more lovingkindness.

Looking back on these women, I might have been called to pray for their finances or for safety, or maybe for Jesus to send her a good friend. Maybe Uncle Albert just needed someone to take the time to go shopping with him; maybe mom could have used another woman to have coffee with her. When I realized that I was being given information to intercede but using it to hurt others, I was embarrassed before the Lord. I repented and began to learn from Him how to respond.

The lesson is this: Any time we take information from God and change it or use it outside His will, we are in sin and in need of repentance and restoration. This is another area

Worrying, *Like Rocking*...

where the answers to our prayers can be delayed.

God created light and darkness, and He created matches and no matches. He gives generously to those who ask, but He, like any good parent, has guidelines for His children. He allows some situations to stretch our faith in Him, such as believing and waiting for the prodigal child to return to Him. Our Father *is* Patience, and is patient, and teaches us patience. Patience keeps us strong in crises, focuses us in sorrow, and creates a testimony to encourage our children and others in the mighty works of the Lord. Our patience in a crisis brings forth a mighty weapon against the enemy. That weapon is faith that can endure the test of time, and our

String of Pearls

testimony of that faith strengthens the next generation.

In the Indiana Jones movie, *The Last Crusade*, Indy is hurrying through caves and tunnels, following a map with ancient writing that uses riddles as clues. His father is dying, and he must find the Holy Grail, since it is the only hope of saving his father. At one point he comes to a great chasm, and the riddle tells Indy that to cross it, he must take a leap of faith. In faith, Indy steps out into the air, and his foot lands on something solid, something he couldn't see from where he stood on the edge. Faith is stepping out on what seems like nothing in the hope of finding something solid there. We can sit in our rocking chair worrying about things, or we can take a step of faith to

Worrying, *Like Rocking*...

seek the One who made it all and has all the answers.

CHALLENGE: In what areas of your life can you more effectively use your time? In faith, what areas of your life are you waiting for God to accomplish something? What do the above questions reveal to you about yourself and Christ?

Chapter 2

I Can Do It *by Myself*

---

*I know the plans I have for you,
declares the Lord,
plans for welfare and not for calamity
to give you a future and a hope.*

Jeremiah 29:11

My parents say that my first sentence was, "I do it mine by self!" This trait has been my weakness *and* my strength. As a teen, being strong willed was my undoing. I used my unseasoned abilities to rebel and argue every chance I found. Not wanting to be told what to do or who I could date created great fireworks of arguments in our home. After all, all the adults I knew had made mistakes, so who were they to tell me what to do? They tried to share the wisdom they'd learned from their own poor decisions, but I would not listen. I wanted to think for myself, and they kept giving me the answers.

In the end, my poor choices hurt not just me, but my parents and, eventually, my children. After my divorce, by the time I hit bottom and began to turn back to God, there was so much for me to ask forgiveness for, and so much I needed Jesus to handle. I had tried everything I knew to fix my life, and nothing worked. As a matter of fact, everything got worse. There was no place left to go for help

I Can Do It *by Myself*

except to the Father, and I began there with confession and repentance.

The most difficult part of asking forgiveness was accepting it from God and from myself. Allowing Jesus to come and clean up the mess I had created was humbling. He did not deserve that. I had made the mess, so why was He doing the dirty work? I lived through the results of my rebellion for many years to come, but I soon learned that I could not live through them alone. Jesus said He would never leave me or forsake me, and I took Him at His Word.

My strong will also worked to my advantage at times. Once I had repented and come back to Christ, my "do it mine by self" attitude changed to "Have it your way, Lord. I will do whatever you tell me."

String of Pearls

Our enemy, that dust-eating, belly-crawling snake, loves to take what God calls *good* and use it for evil. Chapter 3 of Genesis begins, "Now, the Serpent was more crafty than any beast of the field." It seems the writer is trying to bring the reader up to speed with what Adam, Eve, and God already know. We know that God brought all the animals to Adam to name and to determine if any of them was a suitable mate for him. We can draw two conclusions from this information. First, we know that Adam had been around the serpent before the Fall because he had observed it to see if it was a match for him. Second, because he had observed and evaluated it, the serpent knew its characteristics.

In fact, Adam knew that the serpent was crafty, and the serpent knew Adam had his

I Can Do It *by Myself*

number. But perhaps Eve did not know the serpent, so the crafty beast pursued her instead of Adam.

Have you ever wondered why Eve acted as she did? She obviously understood the rules: "From all the trees of the garden you may eat freely but from the Tree of the Knowledge of Good and Evil, you may not eat." That seems simple enough, yet she added to God's rules "you must not even touch" and justified her actions through practicality. "She saw it was good for food." When she went out on her own, she began to doubt God's motives for the restriction.

Have you ever felt that way?

I have.

Satan told Eve that God had an ulterior motive for not wanting her to eat the apple.

String of Pearls

Satan said that if you ate the apple then you would know what God knows, implying that there was deceit on God's part. Eve, in a moment of doubt, uncertainty, and willfulness, listened to Satan. She allowed Satan's words to challenge the authority of God, to remain in her mind, and to influence her to take action.

She took the fruit and ate it.

We have all done something that was wrong on a dare or through willful defiance, haven't we? Drinking under age, riding on the hood of a car just to see if we could hang on the longest, flirting with danger and thinking we would not get caught.

Did Eve's actions come from off the top of her head? Were they an impulsive move? Or could it be that because she ruminated over a matter long enough, her thoughts led to actions

I Can Do It *by Myself*

that she desired and she created the answer that suited her?

Don't we all do the same thing?

The Lord had said to Adam, "From any tree you may eat freely; but from the tree of the knowledge of good and evil you shall not eat, for in the day that you eat from it you shall surely die."

Eve's version was, "From the fruit of the trees of the garden we may eat; but from the fruit of the tree which is in the middle of the garden, God has said, 'you may not eat from it or touch it, lest you die.'" And, as the story goes, the serpent persuaded, the woman ate, and then Adam did the same.

So often we have what I call a "Shake and Bake" mentality. The old commercial showed a young girl meeting her daddy at the door to tell him that dinner was ready, proudly declaring, "And I helped!" Perhaps Eve just wanted to know what God knew so she could help Him.

Regardless of her intentions, the result was rebellion, plain and simple. And it continues to affect each one of us, man and woman, to this day. Instead of going to the One who made everything, the One who walked with her and Adam in the cool of the day in the amazing Garden that He created for them to live in, she chose to listen to the father of lies and do what she thought best.

Let's look in our own lives. What's in our own gardens? It is so easy to get caught up in the wonderful gifts we have in this era: newspapers, magazines, radio, television, cable, computers, and cell phones. These are such amazing times. But, just as it was in the Garden,

I Can Do It *by Myself*

it is so easy for evil to influence our homes before we even realize what has happened, and then life begins to unravel and disintegrate.

Just as in the beginning, it is vital for us to *shamar* our homes, our families, and our minds. Take a few minutes right now and ask Christ to allow you to see what He sees in our gardens. Some of the things you might take a look at could be inappropriate things: books, movies, relationships, emotional affairs;, deceit and lies, or unforgiveness. Some may seem harmless at first, yet allowing negative or deceitful thoughts to linger can lead to actions that we, not God, initiate.

Thus the serpent invades our gardens. Just as Adam was to *shamar* the garden, we are to *shamar* our minds, our homes, and who and what we allow to come near our families. Some

String of Pearls

of us are single mothers, head of our household. We are the front line of protection in our homes. I have been a single mother, and it was the most difficult time in my life. I was the protection and provider for my children. I *shamared* the best I could, but it was Christ who brought us through it all. I could not see Him clearly at the time, but looking back, I see clearly His nail-scarred handprint in my life.

I have seen my car make it to the kids' schools, to work, to the bank, and then to the gas station—when it shouldn't even have gone past the school. Another time money, which had been owed to me for two years, came on the day the mortgage was due. I did not have enough to pay it and not only did I make the payment, but it was enough to buy a few groceries too. He ran off men I did not need to

I Can Do It *by Myself*

be around and handpicked the man I married. He did all this because I told him that I was ready to be stubborn in clinging to His stubborn love.

Think about this.

First, we are to take our instructions from Christ, the living Word of God. Second, after we have received our instructions, we are to take action based on what lines up with the Word of God and prayer. Check what you think God is telling you by looking up a subject in the Bible.

One useful tool I use, which brings new scripture to me I might not find otherwise, is Young's WORD search. I also discuss some of my decisions with trusted friends and ask them to pray with me.

String of Pearls

Encourage yourself with the truth that you are not cursed or abandoned, and that you are not alone. We don't have to take matters into our own hands. He gives us choices and then stays with us through the results, whether we are celebrating or commiserating.

He is always there.

Sometimes He removes the consequences of our sins, and sometimes He stays with us as our advocate as we go through the consequences of our actions.

I have often heard people say that God placed a curse on man because of the Fall. I cannot find in the Bible where God cursed Adam, Eve, or mankind. Genesis 3 says that God cursed the serpent and the ground, not that He cursed His children. But He did give them consequences because of their very poor

I Can Do It *by Myself*

choices. Adam would continue to work and cultivate, but now thorns and thistles would grow despite his work. He would no longer have that deep satisfaction from his work in the Garden or his daily, intimate relationship with God, and Eve's pain in childbirth would increase.

Let us back up and revisit this story. When Adam and Eve's eyes were opened, what was their first action? They sewed together fig leaves to cover their nakedness because they were ashamed and embarrassed. They tried to use the things of this world to cover the wrong they had done. They tried to sew together leaves to cover themselves. Have you ever picked leaves and tried to sew them together? The least little tug, and they tear to shreds. After a couple of days away from the branch, they crumble.

String of Pearls

That is what it is like when we try to cover and conceal our own sin. We cannot redeem ourselves; the little that we are able to do cannot hold up under the pressure and the repeated fiery arrows that come at us from Satan. Our own attempts at redemption crumble, and we continually have to try to redo ourselves, poorly perhaps, and never successfully.

What activated Adam and Eve's instinct to hide?

Shame?

Our enemy wants us to feel shame because shame beats us down. It causes us to hide or to run. The voice of the One who loved Adam and Eve and called to them was not calling to shame them.

I Can Do It *by Myself*

Yes, God causes us to be aware of our state, but He does it so we can repent and turn back to Him. Instead of repenting, Adam and Eve tried to cover their shame and make excuses. The One who loved them so much called, "Where are you?"

Do you think that God didn't know where they were or what had happened? He was asking them for more than their location. He was asking them to look at what was separating them from Him. As my mother would say, "What have you gotten yourself into?"

Satan came and tried to separate them from God, asking questions and setting Eve up to doubt the meaning of what God had told Adam. "Did God really say that? Will you really die? There's something He isn't telling you; there is more," is what the snake has implied.

String of Pearls

Eve began to listen to the voice of the world, to Satan, instead of to the voice of the One who loved her. She made a unilateral decision based on half-truths and self-will.

Satan is good about taking the truth, twisting it, and causing us to doubt the original meaning. 2 Timothy 3:14-15 "You, however, continue in the things you have learned and become convinced of, knowing from whom you have learned them; and that from childhood you have known the sacred writings which are able to give you the wisdom that leads to salvation through faith which is in Christ Jesus." That is why it is so vital for us to know the Word of God for ourselves and teach it to the next generation.

Here is something we all need to be aware of: Satan does not care about us. We mean

I Can Do It *by Myself*

nothing to him. He would not waste his time on us except for one thing: *God loves us.* To hurt God, he comes after us. Think about it. The way to my heart is through my children. When you love them, you touch my heart, but if you harm them, I will become a frightening lioness. Satan knows about, and uses, God's love for us against us.

God came to Adam and Eve asking questions. Where are you? (Have you moved away from Me?) Who told you? (Whose voice are you listening to?) Did you disobey? (Will you acknowledge your actions?)

I remember being in trouble with my parents, and I could always tell by the questions they asked if they knew exactly what had happened and were testing me for the truth, or if they were fishing. Adam and Eve acted like they were a couple of bricks short of a truckload. Sure, they had almost literally been "born yesterday," but they were created as intelligent beings and should have seen this one coming. Our sins will surely find us out!

Eve was not the only one trying to help God. Remember Sarah? God promised Abraham that she would bear him a child. As time passed, Sarah recognized the world's view—that the promise could not come true at her age—and she took on that "Shake and Bake" mentality. Here she was, ready to help God. Well, of course they had not had a baby, she thought. She had not helped God yet. So in came Hagar, and Sarah gave her to Abraham to produce an heir. Wow. Sarah must have been feeling pretty smart. Look at the wonderful plan she came up

I Can Do It *by Myself*

with, one that neither Abraham nor God had thought of!

Have you ever done something or said something that was really dumb, and you couldn't take it back?

I have.

And then I kick myself, saying, "What in the world was I thinking? Oh, yeah. I *wasn't* thinking!" That's what happens when we try to help God without being led by Him. We feel a whole lot of dumb, and we get into a whole lot of trouble. The sad part is, some of these decisions can follow us the rest of our lives and affect many other lives as well as generations yet to come.

Lord, have mercy.

In spiritual warfare this tendency to act without God is called a Jezebel spirit. The

STRING OF PEARLS

Jezebel spirit wants power and control. It wants to dominate men.

In her book *Prayer Portions*, Sylvia Gunter says: "The Jezebel spirit exercises a major role in the power of evil over our nations today. It is in the church and in your family. The spirit of Jezebel seeks to destroy true worship, the family, morality, and the God-ordained role of male authority. It misleads and corrupts the church and seeks to neutralize the life of prophets, pastors, and other male authorities. The spirit is genderless, but seems to work very effectively through women and sensitive male personalities. The only answer for the Jezebel spirit is true discernment, complete "rug-

I Can Do It *by Myself*

eating" repentance, and victory in spiritual warfare."[2]

We've all been around people who must be in control. Things must go their way, or they make our lives miserable. If we're really honest, we know, too, there are times we've been under the influence of a Jezebel spirit. God is calling women into places of authority and preparing us in our spirit and mind for all that we will encounter. But we must recognize that He is the one in control. He is the one who removes boulders and knocks down the doors of bronze and gates of iron. Our job is to be humble and obedient to Him, the Author and Perfecter of our faith. We must be patient, not controlling,

---

[2] Sylvia Gunter, *Prayer Portions*, The Father's Business (1995), 146.

toward others who have not come to the understanding of Christ. God makes all things happen, not us.

The Jezebel spirit will destroy anyone who gets in its way as it tries to establish itself as the controller and supreme authority. Its goal is to leave as many as necessary dead in its wake as it makes its way to the top. In *God's Bold Call to Women*, Barbara Yoder says that the Jezebel spirit moves in a way that is similar to witchcraft and to the Anti-Christ that tries to stop the movement of God. It wants to dominate man and bring glory to itself. This is not a call to the women of God.[3]

Eve was created as Adam's helpmate, taken from his side to partner with him. To help

---

[3] Yoder, Barbara, *God's Bold Call to Women*, Regal Books (2005), 21.

I Can Do It *by Myself*

someone, according to *Webster's New World College Dictionary* is "to make easier, to make more effective, to share in labor." When we give help to someone, we give strength or information that the other person may not have. As women, we are an influencing factor in our families.

We must watch and be careful with the influence we have over others. Like it or not, our men are listening to us. They may not tell us, but they are listening. I love the movie *My Big Fat Greek Wedding*. One of the characters gives us a wonderful paradigm for our job as women. The bride's mother says that the man is the head of the house, but the woman is the neck that turns the head. I love this. This paradigm describes perfectly the great influence we have as women. It is our job to help our men see all they need to see in order to make good decisions.

I adore my husband. Part of what attracts me to him is his brilliant mind, but he is only human, and he needs my perspective. He has a wonderful book education and great logic, but I have my feet on the track with running experience. Together we make a good team. I turn the head to see all the information it needs to make decisions, and pray for his decisions to line up with God's will.

And we women have so much to share with each other through our life experiences—the knowledge we have from doing things the wrong way and then finding a better way. True authenticity among women is a rare treasure, so when we find women who are open and honest about who they are, we gravitate to them.

I Can Do It *by Myself*

Typically they are women who dress well but modestly, not flashy. They have a gentle smile even when they are concerned. They speak wisdom into our lives as well as into particular situations. They are slow to anger, but when they decide that righteous anger is appropriate, stand back! Heads may roll. Yet for the better part of their lives, these women have found the secret to peace that passes understanding. Don't ever think that they are immune to fears and sorrows; they wrestle with them, too. But they have learned to give thanks in all things, to worship through fear, and to trust that Jesus is greater than any enemy we have.

Yes, Eve's desire to make a unilateral decision affects us all to this day. What should be our response?

STRING OF PEARLS

(1) We must acknowledge that all authority belongs to Christ. In Him we can move and have our being, but only in Him. Outside Him, we risk bringing on consequences that could affect generations to come.

(2) We need to check our hearts and repent of any Jezebel spirit that may be destroying our lives and the authority of our husbands.

(3) We must pray for the men in our lives—that they will be the godly men they were created to be, that they will rise up like Elijah and take up the mantle of prayer.

And we must pray for ourselves. Today, find a quiet place and talk to the Lord. Ask Him where He wants you to have authority and where you should let go. I know this: your Father in heaven delights in you. He delights in

I Can Do It *by Myself*

hearing your voice and listening to your thoughts.

He created you perfectly.

Even the things you consider faults, He calls perfectly made, because in our weakness He is strong. Know that He adores you and is leading you in a way to prosper you in your spirit first so you can live to the fullest extent of who He has created you to be. Even a "do it myself" attitude gives Him many opportunities to extend His mercy and grace to us. Even an independent, unilateral thinking woman, like me, can be molded into Christ's image. Boy, am I glad that I am not expected to achieve that one myself!

CHALLENGE: What are some areas of your life where Satan has tried to separate you from

String of Pearls

Christ? What were the consequences? What do you know about God's plans for you? In what ways is He giving you a Hope and a Future?

Chapter 3

Rowing *on the River*

---

*He heals the broken hearted
and binds up their sorrows.*

Psalms 147:3

NOTHING IS MORE DEVASTATING than being betrayed by an intimate friend.

Someone who knows all our secrets.

Someone who shares the same friends and church.

String of Pearls

Maybe it is something small, like your private business running through all those circles. You confided a prayer request to a friend over coffee one morning, only to discover that the entire ball park knows about it before you arrive that afternoon. Maybe a friend at work turned out to be an enemy in sheep's clothing, who took all your work as her own, and received your credit and promotion. Or maybe you walked into work and were the object of razor-tongued women who had chosen you for their "rip-up" target of the day. Perhaps you have experienced a husband running away, or the double whammy of a husband and a friend running off together.

Sometimes life can become so difficult that our faith is shaken and pulled to the point that we wonder if we have the faith to get up and

Rowing *on the River*

face another day! The pain that comes from such a loss is followed by the mental ruminations that can torment us until our last breath if we don't deal with them. We hold on to so much in our hearts and in our minds.

Did you realize that this all began in the Garden of Eden?

Yes, it is part of the consequences God handed down to Eve. She wanted to know what God knew. In learning that, she was also allowed to know the heart of God. She learned, as do all women, the sorrow of a broken heart.

In Genesis 3:14 God says to Eve, "I will greatly multiply your pain in childbirth, in pain you shall bring forth children; yet your desire shall be for your husband, and he shall rule over you." Notice that there was no curse. God did not curse His children, but as any good parent, He handed down consequences that fit the heinous sin of rebellion.

The Lord God said that the pain of childbirth would *increase*, so there must have been a measure of pain from the start. The word *pain* occurs twice in the sentence. The first time, the Hebrew word is *itstsabown*, physical pain, and it can also be translated as sorrow, labor, or labor in childbirth. It is the same word God uses for Adam as he worked the land that was now cursed.

Etseb is the second word for pain. It is a thing shaped or formed, an earthen vessel, labor, toil, trouble, grievance. Matthew Henry Commentary calls this pain a state of sorrow. According to *Webster's College Dictionary*, sorrow means mental suffering caused by loss, disappointment, grief, sadness, or regret. So

Rowing *on the River*

there is not only physical pain associated with childbirth; there is also emotional pain with forming these earthen vessels in the way they should go. Even though raising children causes sorrow, those children are also a source of great joy. We laugh with them as well as cry with them, and we rejoice in their victories as though they were our own.

We live in a fallen world. We all face the consequences of sin, but remember that we have not been left alone. Jesus sent us His Holy Spirit to comfort and guide us through all the sorrow, fears, and tears. Jesus knows it's hard on this side of heaven, and He stays near to help us in our struggle. His goal is not for us to struggle, but through the struggle to enable our faith to grow, and our relationship to grow, into oneness with Him.

String of Pearls

My children are big fans of their computer social networking groups. Looking through the pages of status updates, I see that most people tell about their children, putting up pictures from their past, remembering dates of loved ones who died, and, guess what? Most of these status updates are from women.

Women are the memory keepers in most families. We can remember where we were the night of our first kiss and what our future mother-in-law was wearing or cooking the first time we met her. We treasure our children's first step and first word, and we still cringe over the memory of their first skinned knee. We know our family's favorite food from the honeymoon to the last meal together. Many of us have a jar of teeth that our children lost, because we can't bear to throw them away. We

Rowing *on the River*

can read our children's expressions and know what they are thinking from the time we place them in the cradle to the time they put their first-born in a cradle. We remember everything and treasure all these things in our hearts.

But sometimes we only remember the times things have gone wrong. We need to practice remembering the good. There is an old expression, "Of all the things I've lost, my mind I miss the most." Remembering only the sad times can make us feel like we are losing our minds. We all need to practice remembering the times when God was there and not just the times when everything seems to turn into pumpkins, like Cinderella's coach.

God created our ability to remember for a reason. How would we know that He is moving on our behalf if we could not remember the sorrow or compare it to the solution? How else would we know that our God has not left us alone but is active in our lives? He invites us to review the past so we can see His righteousness and faithfulness from our beginning to our present.

Jeremiah 29:11 says, "For I know the plans I have for you, declares the Lord, plans for welfare and not for calamity to give you a future and a hope." The Hebrew word here for future, *achariyth*, actually means behind. That's kind of crazy, don't you think?

The Hebrew way of thinking was like a man rowing a boat: he backs into the future. What is behind and what is future come from the same root and the same direction. When the patriarchs prayed, they recalled all the things that God had done for His people. They would

Rowing *on the River*

begin with Abraham and bring it up to the present time.

Paul and Peter, when brought before the courts, began their arguments by recalling the facts of God from the beginning.

God wants us to remember our past, so that we can see His hand in motion. For women, remembering the past can be also a source of great sorrow. We remember the disappointments of a life that did not turn out as hoped, a child gone prodigal and our prayers for him unanswered for twenty years. We remember the betrayal of a husband who did not keep the promises he made before God, and we remember asking God to heal a person or relationship where we didn't see any change.

Sometimes other women are part of the sorrow. When we make bad choices, other women can be quick to judge and slow to forget. Because of their memories, women can carry that sorrow and even reproach, possibly for life. Sin brings on the sorrow, but Christ can take this sorrow and bring forth something of beauty. Remember the razor-tongued women who try to destroy other women? They and their victims have at least one thing in common: they have all have been hurt by something in their lives. Someone who is wounded will respond in one of two ways, becoming either a victim or a predator.

Giving our sorrow to Christ and knowing He has heard us in the throne room gives us a third option that the world cannot always comprehend. Our sorrows become mighty tools for Christ, and He allows us to share in

Rowing *on the River*

His joy as we see our prayers of sorrow turned into shouts of joy when the victory is done.

1 Samuel 1:1-18 is the story of Elkanah and his two wives, Hannah and Peninnah. Hannah has her husband's love, but she has no children. Her antagonist, Peninnah, has children but not Elkanah's love. Peninnah provokes Hannah daily over not having children. In that culture it was a thing of great shame, and it still is in some countries. Hannah cried for years, and one year, when the family was at the temple for their annual sacrifice, she got to the point that she could no longer take it. She could not eat; she had been provoked with sorrow by Peninnah. Her husband could not understand why his love was not enough for her; and to add salt to her wound, the priest accused her of drunkenness when she went to pray!

String of Pearls

Hannah was a woman bearing sorrow for something she could not control, and Peninnah might have been operating in the spirit of Jezebel. She looks like she delighted in bringing sorrow to Hannah, perhaps just for sport, or because she did not have Elkanah's love. Maybe she wanted to dominate Hannah and be the head wife of the family.

And men just don't understand sometimes. Hannah could not get a break. The only one who did understand her was the Lord God, who honored her persistence in prayer by giving her a son, and not just any son.

Hannah made and kept a promise she made to Him on the floor of the temple and gave Samuel to the Lord to serve Him for life. As soon as Samuel was born, Hannah broke out in the most beautiful prayer of praise and

Rowing *on the River*

thanksgiving because God did much more than she could have hoped for or dreamed of asking.

The Bible does not tell us how old Samuel was when he was dedicated to the Lord and began to live at the temple. Don't you know that Hannah, like you and me with our babies, treasured everything about Samuel in her heart? She knew every smile, laugh, and tooth coming in, and when they traveled to the temple, she brought him a coat. Mothers never forget, and neither does God. Isaiah 49:15 tells us, "Can a woman forget her nursing child and have no compassion on the son of her womb? Even these may forget, but I will not forget you."

Hannah gave her treasure to the Lord; it was her very greatest treasure, her first-born son. But what she did not realize at the time was that

STRING OF PEARLS

she was giving not just to the Lord, but to the nation of Israel as well. She went through the sorrow of being barren and the pains of birth to rejoicing so greatly that her words were recorded for all generations, then to the sorrow of giving up her only child to God. She had no idea whether or not she would have more children, but she was a woman of great character and faith and received the honor of being recorded in the Word of God. Before she even held her baby in her arms, she was rejoicing in what she knew was a promise from God. She had not seen, but she believed.

The greatest enemy of sorrow is the joy in faith. Hannah believed God and surrendered all she had to Him. God accepted her gift and, through Samuel, brought forth a new day for Israel. Not only did Hannah bear Samuel, but

Rowing *on the River*

she bore a new beginning for Israel, a day when God returned to talking with His people, and Samuel was the conduit for that communication. God longs for us to surrender our sorrows and the things we consider flaws, so that He can make beauty out of what we see as ashes. What we see as sorrows and flaws, He calls perfectly made because He can see the end result. Christ and the Father wait patiently for us to surrender all of our sorrows so that the joy can come in His perfect will.

In 2 Samuel 13, Amnon is consumed by lust and rapes his sister Tamar even though she begs him not to. Then he despises her and throws her out. Tamar does not deserve this; it is a horrible crime against her, and she asks Amnon where she can get rid of the reproach and sorrow that he has placed on her. Their brother Absalom hears what has happened, tells Tamar not to take the matter to heart, and takes her into his home, where she lives desolated for the rest of her life. Then Absalom murders Amnon.

Is Absalom a nut?

Or unfeeling?

Or just incapable of understanding Tamar's despair?

Where is her mother or sisters or friends? Do they not know? Or is Tamar such an embarrassment to the family that they want to sweep it under the rug and allow her to stay hidden? The Bible is quiet about these things, but I think about what she must have gone through to live in such despair.

Despair occurs when great sorrow and devastation leave us speechless and make us

Rowing *on the River*

waste away and ruin ourselves. Now here's the shocker. Tamar, Amnon, and Absalom were King David's children. David is the one whom God called a man after His heart. Yet Tamar wondered where she could go to remove the reproach that she carried—her rape by Amnon and Absalom's murder of Amnon.

Having children can bring great sorrow, as I'm sure these boys brought sorrow to King David. As we carry these sorrows and memories in our hearts, we must learn how to approach sorrow and reproach, to run from the things that destroy, and to trust God to make all things new again. And we must teach the next generation of women how to do these things, too.

Living in a way that we, as women, are genuine, authentic, and truthful about

String of Pearls

ourselves and our lives is so important. We all would love for others to think that our lives are perfect, we have a perfect white-picket fence around our perfect homes, our children are superior, and every day is a good hair day. But when we make those claims, we are lying like a big dog. They are not true. Some may be true, some of the time. But is it right to brag? Is it right to make yourself feel better at the expense of making others feel less?

God has brought each of us through some mighty tough times, and to say differently is wrong. He creates in us His testimony so we can share it, not bury it and tell people that we have always had a great and perfect life. To be honest, I don't want to stand next to anyone telling such tales. Lightening can strike. I can hear the Lord saying, "Don't make me come

Rowing *on the River*

down there and tell the truth!," just as I told my children when I knew they needed to "fess up"—do you want to tell me what happened, or do you want *me* to tell *you* what happened? We always want to tell our side first, because we are kinder to our story than someone else would be.

Am I telling the truth?

The Word tells us, "Greater is He that is in us, than he that is in the world." I believe this is true. When our sorrows bury us alive in despair, reproach, and even great depression, we need to remember that the One who has all the answers resides in our hearts. And if He resides in us, we have the answers we need. Sometimes we may need counselors to help guide us to the truth, and sometimes we can come to the answer if we have a friend who will

STRING OF PEARLS

simply listen to us and remind us of the truth. This may take a long time and a lot of prayer, fasting, and searching the Word. But if we are saved, He is in us and with us.

At one of the most difficult times in my life I was pouring my heart out to the Lord, crying out for His intervention. I was searching everything I could find on fear, marriage, and the Holy Spirit. One day I was reading Acts 8:14: "Now when the Apostles in Jerusalem heard that Samaria had received the Word of God, they sent them Peter and John, who came down and prayed for them, that they might receive the Holy Spirit. For He had not yet fallen upon any of them; they had simply been baptized in the name of the Lord Jesus. Then the Apostles began laying their hands on the

Rowing *on the River*

Samaritans and they were receiving the Holy Spirit."

I remember feeling bewildered about seeing two different acts—being baptized for the forgiveness of sin and acceptance of Christ as savior, and receiving the laying on of hands and the Holy Spirit. I was at the point of such desperation that I was willing to try anything. But I was concerned. I'd heard that people who were spirit filled or baptized in the Holy Spirit rolled down the aisles in church and handled snakes and spoke in tongues. I wasn't sure I wanted any of that. It sounded bizarre even though it was in the Bible. But I was desperate and willing to try anything.

I got on the floor and told God that if He thought this was a good idea for me and would benefit His will for my life, and would help me to embrace His will, then He had my permission to do whatever He thought best. But I did have one request: please don't give me a bunch of emotionalism. I had enough drama in my life and did not need more. That was all I prayed. Nothing happened.

A month later a bunch of friends came over to watch a football game. I had prepared some food for them, but when the get-together became inappropriate, I took myself and my children to the back of the house and closed us off. Again, I got on the floor, pleading with God to help. At one point I looked up, and I could see something that looked like ticker tape moving across the ceiling, so I wrote down the words that appeared.

The first two words were *abba* and *agape*. I thought to myself, "I'm making this up. I

Rowing *on the River*

already know these words." But I continued to write the words I was seeing, and it looked like a sentence. After six years of asking people and trying to look up words I couldn't spell, I finally found the meaning of each word. The sentence was, "The Father's benevolent love for the woman of this house, that she may abide in the shadow of my wings and exult God." I had turned to Christ in my desperation, and He had heard my prayer and answered me with great gentleness, faithfulness, and love.

Perhaps this is a place you might want to stop and ask Christ to give you a greater measure of His Holy Spirit to encourage you and equip you for what is to come as you row into your future. Hannah chose to trust God for her answer, and she found Him to be faithful. Tamar chose to allow her sorrow to consume her. How we respond to our travails is a choice. God gives us a way to redeem all things in Christ Jesus. No matter what has happened to us, or what we have done, or what has happened to those we love, Jesus has a promise for us.

Romans 8:28 says, "We know that God causes all things to work together for good to those who love God, to those who are called according to His purpose." Deuteronomy 20:3b-4 tells us, "Do not be fainthearted. Do not be afraid, or panic, or tremble before them, for the Lord your God is the one who goes with you, to fight for you against your enemies, to save you." And Genesis 50:20 says, "As for you, you meant evil against me, but God meant it for good in order to bring about this present result, to preserve many people alive."

Rowing *on the River*

When we have a past that afflicts us, we carry a heavy weight; when others know about it, sometimes they want to keep us in that spot because it makes them feel safer. Think about a well-off, popular man who finds a poor wallflower woman worthy of his notice, love, and marriage. That can really rattle the cages of women who like having someone they feel superior to. That's what the authority of Christ can do in our lives. He has given us the authority on this earth (Matthew 28:18). He wants us to use it. He expects us to use it and teach it to others and to the generations to come. Jesus wants everyone to see Him through our lives and experience, to see that He is a loving, active, and mighty God who allows that which is unseen to be seen through our lives.

String of Pearls

Let's practice taking our sorrow, memories, and reproach to Jesus to heal. He wants them removed. Holding on to these things can be like wearing a yoke that is too heavy to bear. Jesus came to set us free from the consequences of sin and to defeat that which robs us of our intimacy with him.

CHALLENGE: Make a list of the things you want Him to redeem. Then get into your rowboat, and start looking back at the wonders that He has already done for you and your family. Go as far back as you can remember. If you are fortunate enough to have family members, including grand-parents, you can talk to, ask them to go rowing with you. As you go through your memories and those of your family, look specifically for the situations where you have

Rowing *on the River*

lived with reproach or despair, and pray for the Holy Spirit to come into that memory and heal it. Then look for places where you and your family can see where Christ changed what was a sorrow and created something joyful from it.

CHAPTER 4

Your Testimony, *a Pearl of Great Value*

Those who sow in tears shall reap with joyful shouting. He who goes to and fro weeping, carrying his bag of seed shall indeed come again with a shout of joy bringing his sheaves with him.

Psalms 126:5-6

I BECAME ACCUSTOMED TO SLEEPING WITH THE lamp on and my Bible in the bed with me after someone began stalking me and making threatening phone calls. I would hear noises

String of Pearls

outside, but the police could never find anyone. I had spent so much money trying to secure the house, only to discover that my attempts had been of no help. One night I awoke, and the lamp was on as usual, but I could smell bread baking. I thought I must have been so stressed out that I'd forgotten to turn the oven off, and I ran to the kitchen. It was cold and dark. Nothing was cooking, nothing was turned on, there was no smell of bread. As I got back into bed, I could smell fresh bread again. I told myself that this was God's way of comforting me because fresh bread was served at Sunday dinner with the family all around. I did feel comforted, and I went back to sleep.

A few years later, in my devotional reading, I saw the list of items in the inner court of the tabernacle. Each one was symbolic of Christ.

Your Testimony, *a Pearl of Great Value*

There was the oil that burned at all times; there was a bronze bowl to ceremonially wash the face and hands; there was the curtain that led to the Holy of Holies where the Ark of the Covenant resided; and there was a table on the other side of the Holy of Holies. On this table was placed freshly cooked *shue* bread. *Shue* means presence. The fragrance of the Bread of Presence filled the temple. Christ is the Bread of Presence. On that night many years ago, He came into that room to comfort me. He was so close to me that I could breathe Him in. The Living Word, manna from heaven, let me know He was there in a very tangible way.

The next week someone wrote profanity in my grass with Roundup. As I sobbed in great sorrow and distress to the only One who could help, I felt His presence wrap around me like a bear hug, and I heard Him tell me, "It's misspelled." "What?" I said out loud. I looked, and sure enough, all of the words were misspelled. Again, I heard the Lord speak: "And you're letting this person scare you?" I laughed as hard as I had been crying. That was the day He delivered me from my fear of man and gave me a great trust in Christ.

He may not take us away from the crises of life, but if we only believe, He will deliver us through them. This is part of my testimony of Christ and my faith in Him. I was like the woman with an issue of blood who believed what the Word of the Lord said and trusted in His faithfulness to restore me.

Luke 8:44-46 tells the story of a woman who had an illness that made her bleed for twelve years. Her desperation and faith drove her to

Your Testimony, *a Pearl of Great Value*

do something completely and totally incorrect, both politically and religiously. She touched a man who was not her husband. That was wrong in those times because she was a woman, and an unclean woman at that! "She came from behind and touched the border of His garment. And immediately her flow of blood stopped. And Jesus said, "Who touched Me?" When all denied it, Peter and those with him said, 'Master, the multitudes throng and press You, and You say, "Who touched Me?"' But Jesus said, 'Somebody touched Me, for I perceived power going out from Me.'" Now when the woman saw that she was not hidden, she came trembling; and falling down before Him, she declared to Him in the presence of all the people the reason she had touched Him and how she was healed immediately. And He said

String of Pearls

to her, 'Daughter, be of good cheer; your faith has made you well. Go in peace.'"

Can you imagine having PMS for 12 years? Did they have chocolate in those times? I have to marvel that she was still alive and sane! Leviticus 15:19-33 talks about when a woman has an issue of blood. She is considered unclean. Anyone who sits where she has sat or touches anything she has reclined upon is considered unclean. If she had a husband he may not sleep with her or have anything to do with her, or he becomes unclean. This poor woman had been in that state for twelve years. I can only imagine the sorrow, loneliness, and perhaps hopelessness that were her daily life. She had spent all the money she had and was still not well. Perhaps the reason she was on the street was that she had spent all her money

Your Testimony, *a Pearl of Great Value*

trying to find a cure and found herself homeless.

Notice that Jesus was not looking at her. She was looking at Him, and she recognized that He was the answer. Her faith was so strong that she believed He did not even need to address her, that simply touching His garment could heal her. She reached out and touched the edge of his outer garment. This is so significant. Jesus wore a cloak or robe, described in Numbers 15:38-40. Tassels of blue at the corners of the garment reminded wearers of the Word of God, and wearing the garment every day was a reminder to obey God's commandments. Jesus wore these tassels on his outer garment, and the woman literally reached out and touched the Word of the Lord. The word describing the way she touched the garment is *haptomai*, and it means to fasten oneself to, adhere to, cling to. This woman did not just let the tassel grace her hand; she grabbed hold of it! Many people were crowding in on Jesus, possibly stepping on his robe, pulling at his sleeve. Peter even noted that everyone was pressing in on Him, and He wanted to know who touched Him? Everyone was touching him! But this touch was different. He felt the power go forth. Have you ever prayed and known Jesus was in the room and felt the heat? That's the anointing. It can come in many different ways, however it manifested that day, Jesus recognized the power.

A woman of prayer has power. She grabs the word of God in faith, and Christ takes notice. Isaiah 40:3 tells us, "A voice is crying out, 'Clear the way for the Lord in the wilderness; make smooth the desert a highway

Your Testimony, *a Pearl of Great Value*

for our God.'" This is our assignment as women, to cry out to God, to call Him into the situation.

I have been in prayer ministry for many years, and I have observed that women and men usually pray very differently. Their methods seem to line up with the consequences of the Garden. Men and women can pray for the same problem, but their perspective is usually different. Men pray about the situation and the job that needs to be done, while women pray about how that situation affects the heart. Women hear the sorrow, and men observe the work to be done. When my husband prays, he frequently says, "Let this help us to shine Your light into dark places," and I pray, "Let this draw them closer to You." The Lord has made us different, and together we can cover a situation with a wide range of prayers. If my husband prayed exactly like me, my prayers would be redundant not that redundant is a bad thing. Yet, praying together about the same issue, from different points of view, is of great reward in that we can cover a lot of territory in our prayer life.

As we pray and realize that Christ does hear our prayers and the Holy Spirit is bringing things to mind for us to pray, then our prayer life catches on fire and our faith begins to grow. As Romans 10:17 tells us, "faith comes by hearing, and hearing comes by the Word of God." In other words, faith comes by hearing and hearing and hearing and hearing and hearing the Word of God. The more we hear the Word of God, the more we think about or meditate on it, and the more we meditate on it,

Your Testimony, *a Pearl of Great Value*

the more meaning it has. The more meaning it has, the more we can go boldly before the throne of God to make our petition before Him. When we come before the Lord God, calling His own words back to Him, He cannot deny us because His Word cannot return void. The Word of God fits the prayer. I'm not talking about a name-it, claim-it mentality. That is of this world. But God did say that He would provide for our needs. He is Jehovah-Jireh, our Provider. If we have a need, we can go to Him and pray.

Here is an example of what I mean.

> *"Father, you are Jehovah-Jireh.*
> *You are my Provider.*
>
> *Your Word says You provided for Abraham,*
>
> *You provided for Israel,*
> *and You provide for me.*

String of Pearls

(It's rowboat time now.)

You delivered me from the flu last year when I was sick, and I did not die.

You gave me children when I had none."

And so on. Do you see? When we pray, we recall God's Word back to him. We recall the times when He provided for us, and then we confess. *"Forgive me when I have doubted You, when I did not act as if I believed Your Word was true, for Your Word says that You are not a God who lies. That is a characteristic of our enemy and the world. I can trust that Your Word is true and trustworthy."* Again recalling His word,

Hebrews 6:18 tells us that He cannot lie, and in this I find encouragement.

Your Testimony, *a Pearl of Great Value*

Make your petition before God, and then thank Him even though you do not see the answer right away. You know He has heard you! Psalms 65:2-4 says, "O Thou who dost hear prayer, to thee all men come. Iniquities prevail against me; as for our transgressions, thou dost forgive them. How blessed is the one who thou dost choose and bring near to thee to dwell in thy courts. We will be satisfied with the goodness of thy house, thy holy temple." Also, we have confidence because of what James 5:15-16 tells us: "The effective prayer of a righteous man [or woman] can accomplish much."

Just as the woman with the issue of blood grabbed hold of the *Tzitzit* that represented God's Word, let us grab hold of the Bible and study His Word for the answers we need. Then as we find God's precepts and promises, we begin to pray them—believing what God says and doing it!

Grab hold of the Word of God! This is our weapon of war against our enemy. This was my weapon when I was in fear for my life. I literally saturated myself in the Word of God, day and night. I grabbed hold of it for dear life, and He was there.

Look at Joshua.

God gave him the land to take for Israel, but Joshua still had to go and fight for it! This was no day at the beach, but God was with him.

Joshua 1:3-9: "Every place on which the sole of your foot treads, I have given it to you, just as I spoke to Moses. From the wilderness and this Lebanon, even as far as the great river, the river Euphrates, all the land of the Hittites, and

Your Testimony, *a Pearl of Great Value*

as far as the Great Sea toward the setting of the sun will be your territory. No man will be able to stand before you all the days of your life. Just as I have been with Moses, I will be with you; I will not fail you or forsake you. Be strong and courageous, for you shall give this people possession of the land which I swore to their fathers to give them. Only be strong and very courageous; be careful to do according to all the law which Moses My servant commanded you; do not turn from it to the right or to the left, so that you may have success wherever you go. This book of the law shall not depart from your mouth, but you shall meditate on it day and night, so that you may be careful to do according to all that is written in it; for then you will make your way prosperous, and then you will have success. Have I not commanded you? Be strong and courageous! Do not tremble or be dismayed, for the LORD your God is with you wherever you go."

That is how it is with our prayers to God. Jesus has given us the victory; the land is ours, but it is our job to fight for what is ours. Matthew 11:12 tells us "for the Kingdom of heaven suffers violence, and the violent take it by force." The word for force is *biazo*. It means to seize, carry off by force, claim for oneself eagerly.

We call our military the Armed Forces. They protect the concerns and well-being of the United States. Prayer warriors do the same; we are part of the armed forces of God. And like our country's army, we must learn about and train ourselves in the weapons of war, which for us is the Word of God.

Your Testimony, *a Pearl of Great Value*

Ephesians 6:17 tells us that the Word of God is the sword of the Spirit, a weapon to be used against the enemy. Again, in Hebrews 4:12 we see the correlation between the Word of God and how the Word is a mighty weapon of warfare. When we are filling our minds with the Word of God we are a mighty weapon in the hand of God.

We have a wonderful, loving God who adores us, but there is a point at which he will no longer tolerate stubborn, unrepentant rebellion against Him. He does have a point where His patience will end and righteous indignation will begin. When He gets His Holy dander up, watch out. Heads will roll!

Isaiah 13:1-5: "The burden against Babylon which Isaiah the son of Amoz saw. Lift up a banner on the high mountain, raise your voice to them; wave your hand, that they may enter the gates of the nobles. I have commanded My sanctified one; I have also called My mighty ones for My anger—those who rejoice in my exaltation. The noise of a multitude in the mountains like that of many people! A tumultuous noise of the kingdoms of nations gathered together! The Lord of hosts musters the army for battle. They come from a far country, from the end of the heaven-the Lord and His weapons of indignation, to destroy the whole land."

Barbara Yoder talks about the weapon of indignation. She says this passage shows that both the Lord and His people—His army—have been taken over by a violent spirit. Something has so incensed God and also those who have His heart that they are arising as an army to

Your Testimony, *a Pearl of Great Value*

deal with something that is wrong, evil, and sinful. "In other words, the Lord's weapons of indignation are people. People have become the weapons in His hand. They are being used to open something that is closed off. They are being used to cut off something that has risen up to destroy the nation. Theirs is an indignant spirit, a violent spirit. It rages at something that is totally wrong, something that destroys people's well-being, something that does damage to their ability to thrive spiritually."[4]

We are the army of God when we come against the wrongs we see, the dangers we see, and the fleecing of God's people. Revelation 12:11 says, "And they overcame him [the devil] because of the blood of the Lamb and because of the word of their testimony, and they did not

---

[4] Ibid., 101.

love their life even to death." The blood of the Lamb is God's gift to us. It was His choice and plan for redemption, but the word of their testimony—the testimony of Jesus by His people—is our part in the battle. We cannot testify for Christ without time on the battlefield. Our enemy deceived Eve because she did not stick to the Word of God; she listened to the enemy and embellished.

Know the Word!

We feel mental and emotional pain because Eve chose rebellion over relationship and activated the natural consequence, which is separation from God. She learned what God knew, and that is the sorrow when our children do not obey and instead choose rebellion. And women feel this sorrow not only mentally and emotionally, but physically.

Your Testimony, *a Pearl of Great Value*

Lord, have mercy.

My husband says there are only two things that make someone jump up and move: the sight of blood and the stab of pain. When we feel pain—physical, emotional, mental, or spiritual—what do we do?

Do you run to the phone or to the Throne?

As health care providers, my colleagues and I were certified in emergency care and CPR. The decisions we made in the first few seconds of a crisis could mean the difference between life and death. Ironically, when we practiced CPR, we were always on our knees. When life crises come, we need to drop to our knees, pull out our spiritual arsenal, and go to work.

Being on our knees, pouring our hearts out before the Lord as Hannah did, is the privilege of anyone who intercedes. John 15:13 reminds us that "greater love has no one than this, that one lay down his life for his friends." When we stop what we are doing or put our thoughts on hold to pray for a friend, family member, church, or country, we are doing a kind of laying down our lives.

It is my opinion that the church's greatest sin is not taking advantage of what Christ's death has done for us. We accept suffering as God's perfect will for us. We accept teenage rebellion as just a stage everyone goes through. We accept mental illness as something people have. No, sisters, no! This is not God's perfect will for our lives. Yes, we live in a fallen world, but didn't Christ come to set the captives free? The answer to that would be, *yes*! Didn't Christ say that he came to give life and give life more abundantly? Again, that would be *yes*!

Your Testimony, *a Pearl of Great Value*

We are not taking the territory that his suffering and death provided. Rise up, church, and pray. The land is ours for the taking if we are willing to do the work that His gift provides. Satan knows Christ defeated him, and he is working mightily to kill, steal, and destroy or, at the very least, hide this truth from our eyes.

Rise up, church, and fight!

Paradoxically, our fight begins on our knees. Then, with patience, we wait on our commander-in-chief for instructions. No unilateral moves here, ladies!

Though we are mighty in spirit, we are tender in heart. Many times in my life I have cut through the stronghold of the enemy, bringing my sorrow, using the sword of the Spirit, blinded by a river of tears. On our knees,

String of Pearls

we pray with tears flowing from sorrow. Many times I have cried so hard that I have gone through a whole box of tissues, my sleeves, and the back of my husband's shirt. We have to feel sorry for the first person to hug us after all that!

My precious friend took her granddaughter to see a children's movie in which a cat dies. Now, my friend does not like cats; in fact, she really doesn't like animals at all. But because of some problems that were weighing heavily on her heart, that dying cat received its full share of sympathy. My friend cried so hard that people stared at her. She didn't expect to be crying at the movie; she was not prepared with tissues. She wiped her face with the front of her hand, the back of her hand, the edge of her shirt, and finally the chair itself (won't that make you keep hand sanitizer in your purse?).

Your Testimony, *a Pearl of Great Value*

The granddaughter asked, "Mimi, are you crying about the *cat*?" She knew her Mimi. But God knew Mimi needed a release, and the cat helped to trigger the flow that later led to prayer and the release of her burden.

Did you know that a pearl is pretty much made of oyster mucus, a nice word for snot? An oyster feels pain as a grain of sand cuts into its tender, heart-like tissue, and it coats the sand daily. I never knew I was paying so much for something that sounds so gross. You and I both know that when we get to the point of having the ugly cry going on, the snot flows. As our mucus flows and we come before the throne, covering our sorrows in prayer, something greater than our sorrows is being formed. Our grain of sand is becoming a pearl of great value.

String of Pearls

As we war with the enemy over the territory that is already ours, we allow Christ to create a testimony in us. We cover one sorrow after another with prayer, and the victory is the testimony of what Christ has done.

As we row our boats, facing backwards, we see that our life is a string of pearls. Pearls made up of years of praying for our prodigal child who one day comes back to Christ; for the salvation of a loved one who finally gets it; for the child with a learning disability, finally reading. The Bible tells us that the Gates of Heaven are made of a single pearl. That is one heaping big pearl! How apropos that the entrance to heaven is through a treasure of great value, one made from pain, sorrow, and mucus.

Your Testimony, *a Pearl of Great Value*

CHALLENGE: What causes tears and mucus to flow in your life? In your quiet time, create a prayer to the Lord, call on His name to take a rowboat ride with you. Bring your heart's sorrows to the only one who can make a difference. Write down your prayer and keep it in your Bible. When you begin to see change, document the date and what you see on the back page of your prayer.

CHAPTER 5

Hold on to Your *Pearl of Great Price*

Hope deferred makes a heart sick;
But desire fulfilled is a tree of Life.

Proverbs 13:12

IT WAS THE 1992 SUMMER OLYMPICS IN Barcelona, Spain. Derek Redman from England was the favorite to win gold in the 400-meter race. But 250 meters from the finish line Derek began to limp, and then he fell to the ground. He had pulled a hamstring and was rolling around on the ground in great pain. As he watched the other runners pass him, he knew there was no hope for winning any medals, much less the Gold medal.

The cameras panned out to show the stretcher bearers running to Derek as he pushed himself off the ground and hobbled towards the finish line. A man pressed through the crowd, making his way to Derek. It was his father. Mr. Redmond put his arms around his son to hold him up. "Son, Son," he said. "You don't have to do this."

"Yes I do. I have to finish," Derek cried, as he put one arm around his father and wiped tears with the other.

"Then we go together," determined his father.

The stretcher bearers tried to persuade Derek to quit and let them take him away.

Hold on to Your *Pearl of Great Price*

"No," his father said. "He is going to finish," and he waved the bearers away as if they were flies.

A few yards from the finish line, Mr. Redman let go so that Derek could cross the line on his own. The stadium was on its feet, cheering him on.

If Derek had given up and decided that it was too hard, or too painful, or would take too long, this story would have never been remembered. He might have just been a disqualification on a score sheet. He would have been just another injured athlete in a competition. Instead, he was remembered for his heroic final effort! No, he did not get the *Gold* that he wanted, but he was honored for the *Goal that he achieved*. In a crisis he did not give up just because it was not the end that

String of Pearls

he had hoped for. He finished the race with all that he had in him. Now he is a motivational speaker. He encourages others to press through the hard places.

He never ran again, but God had given him a new passion, one that provides long-term gratification: encouraging and motivating and molding the next generation. Not a short term race, but a long term journey.

Have you ever had a prayer that took too long to be answered or seemed too painful to hold on to? I did. I prayed with everything I could that God would heal my first marriage, and create a testimony for His glory in us. This went on for years, with my life spiraling down and leaving me and our two children in the wake of the worst experience of our lives.

Hold on to Your *Pearl of Great Price*

God did answer my prayers, but it was nothing like I had dictated to him. God rescued me from a bad situation and placed me in a marriage with a wonderful, godly husband. Not that this marriage has been easy; stepfamilies are not for the weak of heart or for those who must have complete order or control. That just isn't going to happen.

I have heard it said that God will not give us more than we can handle. I cannot find this precept in scripture. What I have found, though, is God calling ordinary people to step out of their own ability and do extraordinary things—things that could happen only when a living God is working through someone who is open. It is in that place between "I can do nothing else" and "It is finished" that we see God's glory in ways that could not be seen any other way. Stepping into that for which we seem ill-equipped also strengthens our faith when we see God opening doors that we could not open for ourselves.

God has frequently placed me in situations where I had no choice but to cling to Him with all my might and trust Him. In return, He took me to places in Him and in this world where I could never venture on my own. It is in the area between our own limitations and God's mighty answers that we see our ideas of Christ change and where we begin to grow in our faith and in our likeness to Christ.

It is so tempting to quit and let the stretcher bearers just come and take us away when the pain and sorrow set in. But when we press through the pain, lean on the Father, and refuse to give up, we make it to the goal to partake in

Hold on to Your *Pearl of Great Price*

the victory that Christ won on the cross and share in His Glory. This is the place where the world sees Christ in us.

I have given up so many times, only to get up and continue the fight for God's things. I have been on the floor, crying so hard that I cannot cry anymore so many times, and yet the storm still rages.

Our enemy would love for us to quit praying and stop fighting for our families, friends, country, and churches. Our enemy would love us to give up. That would make his job easier. He says things like, "Why do you believe? Did God really say that?" or "You're going to look like a fool in front of everyone when it never happens," or "You need to do something else and quit looking for God."

String of Pearls

The truth is that we should get up and try our best, leaning on the Father to work though our weak, frail state and let Him accomplish His miracles through us. When we are weak, we are less likely to try to "help" Him. Remember 2 Corinthians 12:9? "My strength is made perfect in weakness."

There are times when prayers seem to be just hitting the ceiling. There have been times when I thought about quitting because I wondered whether God was just going to do what God was going to do anyway. But I was playing right into the enemy's hand. The Word says that He will never leave us or forsake us. Despite tears, pain, or length of time, never give up. Our Father in Heaven is with us. We are the ones He adores. He wants to be with us through this life to show us Himself and to protect,

Hold on to Your *Pearl of Great Price*

defend, and help us achieve all we are meant to be.

I've heard people say, "Don't pray until you are through. Pray until you pray through." Pray past the pain into the victorious healing. Pray past the finite to the infinite. Pray past the limited to the unlimited abundance! When we pray, we are to come alongside of God. We are to be a part and to partner with His perfect will. Praying "Thy will be done" does not mean we fully understand God's plan, and it doesn't mean that we give up.

It is like this. When our sorrows multiply, we want to do more than help God, right? We want to get down into the problem and kill the beast, not just pray. Right? That is human nature. But in wanting to move in the physical, when God has not given us permission, is putting ourselves in His place, not partnering with Him. We're giving greater importance to our plans, timing, abilities and instead of to God's plans, timing, and abilities, thus creating an obstacle to His answering our prayers and healing our sorrows.

Though Isaiah 14:12-14 is probably talking about King Nebuchadnezzar, some theologians believe it could also reveal the thoughts of Satan before he was hurled out of heaven, as well. Satan wanted what he wanted and placed his desires against and above the will of God.

Does that sound painfully familiar? Ouch!

I'm not crazy about seeing myself written down in black and white. We talk about the evil of Satan, but sometimes we act more like him than like our Father in Heaven. As my mom would say, "That's the pot calling the kettle

Hold on to Your *Pearl of Great Price*

black." If God is not answering our prayers, perhaps it is because we are placing our plans and desires above His.

Have you ever worked your will instead of willing His work? I have, and that's a difficult road to backpedal on. When we desire our own way of righting the wrongs or healing the sorrows, we begin to look like Adam and Eve sewing fragile leaves together that can only work for a few hours. Ecclesiastes 12:13, "The conclusion, when all has been heard, is: Fear God and keep His commandments, because this applies to every person." We should be allowing God to come and cover us with the Lamb's skin that will last for generations. Our part is to know the Word of God and obey what it says. Frequently God's ways go against the world and against our human nature. He wants us to partner with Him, not strive against Him.

How do we know what God's will is for us? That is a life-time pursuit that begins with the desire to know Him. What does God want you to do? Micah 6:8, "He has told you, O man, (woman) what is good; and what does the Lord require of you but to do justice, to love kindness, and to walk humbly with your God?" God wants us to come into relationship with Him and to show that relationship to others so that they too can come into relationship with Him. Our obedience, working for justice, showing His love and kindness to others and seeking him will bring us into His will.

But, if we demand our own way, God will allow us to have it. It is not His perfect will, but His permissive will. And He knows that we will

Hold on to Your *Pearl of Great Price*

eventually come to Him to "fix it." Trying to do it ourselves just postpones the answers and brings on greater sorrows and discouragement, and sometimes it even causes us to give up. God in His loving way allows us to try it on our own and then welcomes us back with open arms. He welcomes us, yet He may allow us to suffer the consequences of our actions to help us remember what it is like to be out of His will.

Any time we see Babylon in the Bible, we know that something has gone wrong with God's people. When Babylon is mentioned, we see stories of rebellion, captivity, death, and destruction. Israel has moved out of the will of God. In Revelation 17, we see the woman Babylon with many articles found in the Temple of God, but something there, the pearls, was not in the Temple.

String of Pearls

I think these pearls can be symbolic of our prayers. Prayers and sorrows that we give up on, thinking we will never see the answers. We give up, thinking that we will never see God's redemption in that situation. We give up, and perhaps believe, that it is God's will for us to suffer. When we give up, I believe our enemy holds up our sorrows and claims them as his own trophies, keeping us from using them as the victory and testimony of Christ.

In Revelation 18:20, we read about the woman Babylon, but God has commanded that His people are to rejoice because He has pronounced judgment for us, His beloved, against her, our enemy.

God's will for His children is for good, not evil. What the enemy has stolen, God will restore one day.

Hold on to Your *Pearl of Great Price*

So for the sake of your testimony, don't surrender your treasure, your pearls—your answers to prayer—to the enemy. Hold on! Sometimes answers seem painfully slow in coming (as if we need any more pain!), but they are coming.

In Daniel 10:10, an angel comes to comfort Daniel, who is living as a captive of Babylon, and to bring him the answer to his prayer. The angel tells him that his prayers were heard from the first day, but a prince of Persia opposed him. This was not a flesh-and-blood prince; this was a dark, demonic force that was trying to prevent the answer to his prayer from being delivered.

There is a spiritual war going on around us.

Ephesians 6:12, reminds us that "our battle is not against flesh and blood, but against the rulers, against powers, against the world forces of this darkness, against spiritual forces of wickedness in heavenly places." These are the things that set themselves against God, Christ, and His great passion, which is us. Our enemy seeks to destroy God's authority and set himself as the one to worship. Satan would like to supplant and replace God's kingdom with his own. So he tries to stop God's will for us. We are created in God's image, and I suggest, when Satan sees God's people, seeking Him, His guidance and His will, then Satan sees all that he desires slipping away. We are the heirs and we will inherit all that is God's. (I read the end of the book…we win!) God will answer our prayers, maybe not exactly as we have prayed, but He does answer His children. And sometimes we must battle along side of God in prayer and worship, truth and obedience. He calls us to partner with Him in achieving the answers. 1Corinthians 3:6 "I planted, Apollos watered, but God was causing the growth." We work together with God to achieve what needs to be done according to His will and plans for us. It is God who causes the work to flourish with man.

Throughout the Bible, God is working with man to accomplish all that concerns us and His will for us. He does not need us to accomplish His plan and will. He proved that with the creation of everything there is, and was, and is to come! I do not fully understand why the great, I AM, would want to work with and partner with such an obviously brain damaged people. But He does.

String of Pearls

In the book, *When Heaven Invades Earth* by Bill Johnson,[5] he writes, "God has apparently given himself a self-imposed restriction to act in the affairs of man in response to prayer. God has chosen to work through us. We are His delegated authority on planet earth, and prayer is the vehicle that gives occasion for His invasion."

God chooses to work though us. As we pray and spend time in prayer with Him we develop an intimacy with God. As our intimacy grows our authority from Him, as a trusted friend of God, increases and flows more freely. The result is a partnership with God that moves mountains. I could write a whole book on this subject, but not today.

---

[5] Bill Johnson, *When Heaven Invades Earth*, Treasure House, an imprint of Destiny Image Publishers, Inc, Shippensburg, PA, (2003), 64.

Hold on to Your *Pearl of Great Price*

God wants to answer our prayers with the promises He has given to us, for He is a God who created order out of chaos, light out of darkness, and hope out of despair. I'll take a second helping of that! Thank you very much! Romans 8:28 reminds us, "And we know that God causes all things to work together for good to those who love God, to those who are called according to His purpose." In 2 Peter 3:9, we see some of what is going on when it seems God is taking too long. He is working together for good in our prayers. "The Lord is not slow about His Promise as some count slowness, but is patient toward you, not wishing for any to perish but for all to come to repentance."

The word "promise" is *epaggelia*, a legal term denoting a promise that is undertaken. It is a promise made, with emphasis on the

String of Pearls

promise fulfilled. The promise is placed there as a marker, for the answer.

I worked for twenty-five years in the dental field, and I saw many dental restorations. Many of us have crowns in our mouths today. When something goes wrong with a tooth, the dentist cuts out the bad part (usually leaving us sore for a few days), then makes an impression of the tooth so a lab can make the crown for it. A temporary crown is placed on the tooth. That is a marker for the new crown. It denotes the place where the promised crown will go. Then the lab brings all of the necessary things together and we wait since they do not usually work with just our impression; they work in batches to get the most done for the greatest number of people. The process takes time.

Hold on to Your *Pearl of Great Price*

While we wait, we learn to take it easy on that area of our mouth and allow it to heal. Maybe we read more or hang out with the family more, but we don't do a lot of physical activity because we don't want to get that area bleeding again. We want it to heal as we wait on the promised crown. And the lab works hard to return our crown as soon as possible, knowing that waiting is difficult and the promised crown will be much better and stronger than the temporary one that is marking the place. It is the same with God when we pray.

God does not hold back the answers or promises to our prayers as a cruel person might. But during the time of waiting He engages with us, and teaches things that we would never experience with Him if we were not desperately seeking Him with our whole

String of Pearls

heart. We need to allow Christ to teach us about Himself so that at the point of answered prayer we emerge looking like, acting like, and scented with the fragrance of Christ.

Archbishop Francois Fenelon prayed, "Lord, I know not what I ought to ask of you. You only know what I need. You know me better than I know myself, O Father, give your child what he himself knows not how to ask. Teach me to pray. Pray yourself in me."

As we persevere, sometimes through sorrow, to the answer of His perfect will, our treasured pearl, our sorrow, is brought to fruition and made into something of great value to the world. Our testimony is of greater value than a pearl and stronger than the forces of hell itself.

Never give up.

Hold on to Your *Pearl of Great Price*

What is your favorite worship song? Does it contain a scripture? Write the words down on a 3x5 card and meditate on them this week. If you don't have one, here is one of my favorites.

"Eagle's Wings," written by Reuben Morgan and sung by Darlene Zschech, is based on Isaiah 40:31: "Yet those who wait for the Lord will gain new strength; they will mount up with wings like eagles, they will run and not get tired, they will walk and not become weary."

The song tells how we should be waiting for the Lord—not just sitting in one place staring at the four walls. This kind of waiting has expectation; it's like waiting for Christmas morning. Waiting for the thing you want most; Worshiping, expecting Him to be present with you. This song calls us to wait, with expectation to know Jesus more, to wait on a life closer to

String of Pearls

Him, and a wait where He comes in and lifts you up above the problem, on eagle's wings.

When I let go of all that tries to bury me in temptation, frustration, or sorrow, I need to get away and worship. Then the peace that passes understanding, raises me up on eagle's wings, and calms my troubled heart.

CHALLENGE: Reading God's Word, faith, perseverance, and allowing Him to teach us through the situation, are capabilities mentioned in this chapter to help us overcome and endure our sorrow to the end. Explain what each of these capabilities does to help you through your sorrows.

Chapter 6

Straighten Up *and Fly Right*

It is not I who lives, but Christ in me.

Galatians 2:20

After a divorce from a long and very difficult marriage, a betrayal by someone I thought was a friend, dealing with a stressful job and two very strong-willed teens, I was at the end of my rope, emotionally, physically, and financially. I had lost all hope in God, in people, and in myself.

String of Pearls

I was ready to die.

The only prayer I had left to whisper was, "God, I'm tired."

I began to plan my death.

Little by little I collected prescriptions from doctors until I had enough to do the job.

I am really ashamed to tell this about myself, but each time I talk about it, I find so many women who have either tried to end their lives or contemplated death.

I am thankful to tell you that I did not take the pills.

I eventually flushed them down the toilet.

One day I woke up to my son pulling on my arm. "Come on, Mom. Get out of bed. I need you." What we will not do for ourselves, we will do for our children. That was the day I chose to live. I still did not want to be here, but I could not bear the idea of either of my children or anyone else in my family finding me and having their lives destroyed or, even worse, copying my action.

The sorrows of this life can be so overwhelming. I truly believe that Jesus sent my son into my room that morning because I was close to finishing the job that the divorce had started. But I chose to obey the call He gave through my son. When my son moved away soon after, my daughter and I grew closer, and now we are the best of friends. At the time, she was very young, and I thought she was not very aware of what was going on. I was wrong. To this day we share little details of those dark days.

This was my first experience at dying to my own will and getting up and living for Christ's

String of Pearls

will. It was physically, mentally, and emotionally painful to let go of what I desired. But giving up my own desire for Christ's desire—literally having my will placed on the cross to die, and allowing the new life from and in Christ to take over—gave me the freedom from my past and the joy in life that I had been wanting. Christ died for me to have new life, not just in the life to come, but in this life as well.

Though the dark days were horrible for me and my family, others have had even more sorrow than I experienced or could imagine. *The Secret Holocaust Diaries*, by Carolyn Tomlin and Denise George,[6] is the story of Nonna Bannister. Nonna was a young girl in

---

[6] Denise George and Carolyn Tomlin, *The Secret Holocaust Diaries*, Tyndale House Publishers (2009).

Straighten Up *and Fly Right*

1942, when she and her mother left Russia to work in the German factories because there was no food where they were living. They were packed into cattle cars with other women doing the same thing, and their conditions ranked only slightly above those of the Jews Nonna discovered in the cattle cars at the end of the train. Nonna's heart was saddened by a thin boy, about four years old, with dark, sunken eyes, and she decided to give that little boy her piece of bread.

As she gave the boy her bread, the doors to the cattle cars were opened, and all the people were herded to an open field. Nonna was caught up in the rush. With baton-swinging guards and dogs chasing them, Nonna and the Jews ran into the field to a trench being dug by Jewish men. Cold rain began to fall as the guards told the men to strip off their clothes, and then the guards shot them. The men fell into the grave they had dug. The guards then told everyone else to line up facing the ditch, and they walked down the row, shooting people, execution style, in the back of the head. Nonna was standing with the four-year-old, Nathan, and his mother.

As the guards approached, Nathan pushed Nonna into the ditch. Nonna heard Nathan's mother scream his name, and then she felt his frail little body fall on top of hers, still holding the bread she had given to him. Covered in mud and blood, Nonna did not dare move. She played dead. Once the guards left and everything was quiet, Nonna raised her head, climbed out of the grave, and made her way back to the last place she'd seen her mother.

Straighten Up *and Fly Right*

Nonna Banister was given a second chance at life. The enemy's judgment of her unworthiness could not be completed. They believed Nonna was dead because she was covered in someone else's blood. They ignored her because she was covered by blood and she behaved like one who was dead.

She got a second chance at life.

She didn't have just the hope of a good life; she received a testimony of Christ's provision in her life during horrendous times. Her father, brother, and mother were murdered by the Germans, even though they were Russian Orthodox Christians, not Jews. They were not spared, but she was. God's ways are difficult to understand, but maybe one day we will have an answer to our questions of why such things can happen. Or better yet, when we are with Him and reunited with our loved ones, then the whys really will not matter or need answering. But for here and now, the unanswered questions are difficult to deal with.

I have a friend whose son had been rebellious. He was into drugs and running hard and fast from the Lord. Through her prayers the prodigal son returned home. This young man became an evangelist. Some of his tactics for Christ were to go to a restaurant, eat, pay for his meal. Then as he got up to leave he would pause at the door and give a quick loud message of God's love for them and call them to accept Christ as their Savior. Then he would scoot out the door before he was removed!

His family was strong in their faith and were, as the book of Micah stated, working for justice. One night their son did not come home.

Straighten Up *and Fly Right*

A full scale search was launched to find him. After several days he was found. His car had left the interstate and crashed in such a way that was difficult to see except by air. There were whispers of foul play because of some of the stands his father had taken. Nothing was ever proven.

I listened to his mother tell about all that happened before, during the days of searching for him and after the wreck. Through her sorrow her faith never wavered. She never showed or spoke anything about being mad at God. Her one comment that stayed with me was this, "I don't ask God, 'Why'" His ways are so much higher than mine—that I would never fully understand. So why ask why? I trust that He is God, He is still on the throne, and my son is with Him." My friend was not just saying pretty words, this woman truly believed this and it went all the way down to her core! Sometimes we are not going to have our "whys" answered in this life.

Mary and Martha were probably wondering why Jesus delayed coming to save their sick brother. Jesus could have made it in time before Lazarus died, but He chose not to. Even if Jesus had tried to explain it to His friends ahead of time, they probably would not have understood. I do not think these precious women were much different from us. If Jesus came and told me that someone I loved was going to die in three days, but He would bring her back, I probably would have heard the first part and not listened to the rest. My heart would not have been able to go any further at that point.

Straighten Up *and Fly Right*

The shortest verse in the Bible, "Jesus wept," tells us what happened when Jesus got to Lazarus. Why did He weep? He had allowed Lazarus to die so He could increase people's faith. He was showing them an example for when it came time for Him to die. He was giving them a visual prophecy of what was to come. But that should have been joyful, so I ask why He was weeping. He was weeping not just *with* the people, but also *for* the people. *Wesley's Explanatory Notes*, explains that Jesus was weeping for the great misery sin had brought to mankind.[7] He wept because the ones He loved were in so much pain and sorrow. Jesus was fully God and fully man. He also wept from a human perspective over the

---

[7] John Wesley, *Explanatory Notes Upon the New Testament*, London: Thomas Cordeux (1813), 303.

String of Pearls

death of a friend. Don't we cry when the ones we love are crying? Even if their pain or sorrow does not directly affect us, even if we know it will be okay in the end? We all do.

The word for the people's weeping is different from the word for Jesus' weeping. The word for the people's weeping is *klaio*, which means to bewail and lament. They were on the ground, crying their hearts out. They were crying with no hope of seeing Lazarus again in this life. But the word for Jesus' weeping is *dakroo*, which means to shed tears. Jesus cried with the knowledge and hope of what was to come. He cried because His beloved bride was in mourning. The sorrow that sin brought into the world touched His heart and brought tears to His eyes.

Straighten Up *and Fly Right*

Sorrow is part of this world, and there is no escaping it. The greatest sorrow we will face is the sorrow of death, and sometimes it seems more than we can ever survive. Yet somehow we do survive, even though we are forever changed by the love of, and the absence, of someone who had been a part of our lives.

Even when we know that person is saved, the pain is often unbearable at first. Nothing can prepare us for the death of a loved one, nothing. Even when we know it is coming, there is no way to prepare ourselves to make the pain less.

Jesus came to the earth, lived the life of a man, and chose to die. He lived a life but actually required two deaths, one to life itself and one to self in this life. He did not come so that He could understand us better. God made us, for heaven's sake, so He knows us well, better than we know ourselves. Jesus came so we could know Him better. So that which was unseen could be seen. So the mortal could embrace the immortal. So that which was dying without a choice could have the choice of living a new life. We can live a new life in this world and the world to come because we are covered in someone else's blood, if we repent and obey His commandments. That is the truth of death and *leaving* this world, but what about death and *living* in this world?

I sent out an email to fifty-seven people asking them this question: "Galatians 2:20 says, 'It is not I who lives but Christ who lives in you.' What does that mean to you, and what does that look like in your day-to-day life?" Here are some of the responses.

Straighten Up *and Fly Right*

Hope, who runs a preschool for low-income children and mentors the parents, said, "The first thing that comes to my mind is my journey in the Chi Rho Kids' Ministry. When I enter the doors of church each morning to teach the children or work with the parents, there is no doubt the passion, love and energy that comes from my body is NOT me. I truly am a vessel that Christ is operating out of. The Lord is the driving force of all that happens. I continually pray that we empty ourselves and allow Christ to work miraculously in the children's lives. Year after year I'm amazed at what He does. If it weren't the Lord, there's no doubt my drive and commitment would have weakened by now."

Donnie wrote, "For me it means to surrender our will to God's each and every day .

. . to really mean it when we pray, "Thy will be done." Which is much easier said than done most days."

Angela wrote, "Dying to self every day, putting God's plans and purposes and will first. What it looks like every day . . . well, if you are actually doing it, then it looks like Jesus!"

The one who made me laugh out loud was Hal because his answer shows so much transparency and truth. Hal is a brilliant man who teaches Sunday school to teens, is a lawyer by day and a data systems supervisor for a large insurance company at night. I can brag on him mostly because he is my brother. He wrote, "I feel bad because I always get caught up in everything I am doing and forget that point."

I think we all sometimes realize the same thing Hal does. Oh, yeah, it's not supposed to

Straighten Up *and Fly Right*

be me; it's supposed to be Christ! There are some days when my testimony of Christ, my pearl of great value, looks more like a string of thorns instead of a string of pearls. Dying to self is tough! My *self* is not fond of dying. In fact it does all it can to *not* die.

Francis Frangipane says in his blog, "We can be assured that each step deeper into the Lord's Presence will reveal areas in our hearts which need to be cleansed. Do not be afraid to see yourself as you are. For the Holy Spirit shows you your sin, He comes not to condemn, but to deliver."

He comes to deliver us because we cannot deliver ourselves and because when this happens, our faith is increased, and we are able to tell others how much the Lord loves and to give evidence of that Love.

String of Pearls

When we choose to live by the spirit, we begin to see a change in our lives by listening to the Holy Spirit who dwells in us. Out with the old, and in with the new, filling our minds with God's Word each and every day. It's like coffee in the morning. I like strong coffee to wake up with in the mornings. It helps me to straighten up and fly right. I tell my husband, who is a morning person and likes to talk about deep and serious things before 6:30 a.m., "Don't expect me to respond to anything before coffee. Otherwise you are talking to an inarticulate, and seemingly unintelligent person, so it is not a fair debate! You may win, but it will be a sad win because you were up against an unarmed person." Now, pass the coffee . . . please.

Think about the Word of God like a cup of coffee. It cranks our engine to face everything

Straighten Up *and Fly Right*

coming at us in our day. We can choose to believe what the Word of God says over what we see in our circumstances. The Word of God powers up my day, and then when a situation arises that fits the Word I read earlier, I am energized.

When we believe that God can do what He says He can do and that He is actively working for us, then we have the mind of Christ working in us, whatever the situation. We should consider asking God to reveal Himself through the sorrows in our lives instead of asking him to remove those sorrows. Maybe we have been asking Him for the wrong things all these years. Maybe the question is not "why," but "what" and "where." What does this mean, Lord? Where are You in this problem? What do I need to know about this? What does your

STRING OF PEARLS

Word say concerning this? Where should I begin telling of your love? This is what Galatians 2:20 is saying to me. When I allow Christ to activate the Word of God in me, then it is no longer me living and working in my own strength; it is Christ in me. The Word of God is Christ!

Unless we set our minds on Christ and not this world, we are no better than Adam and Eve trying to cover themselves with leaves and then hide. Are we really trying to remove our sin and sorrows, or are we just trying to cover them so that we look like the world and can fit in better? Death to self means we need to be covered in blood, not leaves, and not our own blood—it's not good enough. We need to be covered in someone else's blood. To die to self as Christians, we must be covered in the blood of

Straighten Up *and Fly Right*

Jesus, and we need to allow His work on the cross to cover and remove our sins. Then as we read God's Word and listen to Him in prayer, our old self begins to die off, and the new self, the one who looks more like Christ, begins to take over.

As we live our lives and live *in* our spirit and in His truth, our flesh and all of its desires, emotions, and rebellion become weaker. This takes time, and it is a daily battle we each face. This is the cross we carry each day with Christ. The full passage of Galatians 2:20 says, "I have been crucified with Christ; and it is no longer I who lives but Christ who lives in me; and the life which I now live in the flesh I live by faith in the Son of God, who loved me and delivered Himself up for me."

String of Pearls

We can live in the life to come and in this life, because we are covered in someone else's blood.

CHALLENGE: What does Galatians 2:20 mean to you, and what does that look like in your day-to-day life? What areas of your life do you struggle in the most? What plan of action will you take to cause that area of your life to die? Are you looking like Jesus?

CHAPTER 7

A New Persona—
From Rags to Riches

*And it was given to the Bride to clothe Herself
in fine linen, bright and clean;
for the fine linen
is the righteous acts of the saints.*

Revelation 19:8

I REMEMBER EVERYTHING ABOUT THE DAY MY husband asked me to marry him. It was June 6, the two-year anniversary of our first date. The sky was clear blue, and the temperature was in the upper 80s as we picked up my parents and

String of Pearls

his children to go for a day at the lake. After a few hours of swimming and riding jet skis, Joseph asked me to go for a walk. We walked up a woodsy dirt path, with the fragrance of pine and moist earth filling the air. We came to a tree that had always caught my attention. It was scarred from many storms and from branches of other trees falling on it. Yet each year it was the first tree to put forth beautiful purple flowers whose light fragrance filled the air and declared that spring had arrived. Part of the trunk bulged out with a colony of little critters living in it, causing its natural upward growth to move laterally to accommodate the new family.

Down on one knee my husband went.

I bent down too, thinking he was going to show me something in the rich compost of

A New Persona—*From Rags to Riches*

leaves. Then he smiled, pulled out a small box, and asked, "Will you?" After a few minutes of joyous words—and acceptance—we walked back to the house to share the news.

Looking back on that day and the tree that marked our words of commitment to our future together, I see that tree as a symbol of what was to come. Many more storms were to come into our lives. Step-families are tough, not for the tender of hide. If you could open Joseph and me up, you would see many scars from being in the line of fire when others were hurting, from others we have caught in their fall, and from storms we weathered. Our trunks and branches are bent and gnarled from accommodating others. Yet just as that tree does, we seem to bring forth beauty out of the difficulties. Hopefully, others see and are encouraged, and hopefully they see Christ in us and know that all things are possible in Him. But even with Christ, it has been hard. Even praying each and every day, there have been times I felt like the Queen of Hearts in *Alice in Wonderland*. I want to lose patience and yell, "Off with their heads!"

I am now going to go ahead and ask the question that most of us, if we are honest with ourselves, have wondered since the resurrection of Christ. If I have new life in Christ and I am a new creation, then why am I still struggling with so much sorrow and sin?

It is true that we have new life in Christ, but we are still in the old body, moving through the war zone. Our spirit and our flesh fight each other for ruler-ship. Our earthly desires need to die, but they don't want to die. If the sign says,

A New Persona—*From Rags to Riches*

"Don't," our flesh yells, "Do!" I know this is a struggle in my life. Even as Christians, we struggle in the flesh with the desires that the world offers—desires for things like gossip.

Sometimes I really would like to listen to the latest talk!

For others it may be drugs or alcohol, stealing, anger, adultery, pornography, etc. Wanting what we want, no matter the cost, is the strong drive of our flesh. When we give in to the desires of this world, we destroy our testimony of Christ in our lives, we destroy ourselves, and we destroy others. Pursuing our desires creates collateral damage, and we notice these choices of the flesh most clearly when we are on the receiving end of that collateral damage.

String of Pearls

This is the point where I need God to send the instruction manual because I have obviously put this life project together the wrong way, and I need Him to come in and clean this mess up for me. How do I get myself into such messes? The better question is how do I get myself out of this and survive? We live in a fallen world, and the only way to survive this is to allow our Savior to come in and save us in it, through it, and from it.

Look at Nehemiah 1. The children of Israel have been captives of the Babylonian empire for seventy years, and then there's a regime change. When the Persians take over, Nehemiah asks his brother about the state of the Jews who escaped and are living in Jerusalem. The report to Nehemiah says that the walls of the city are broken down, the gates

A New Persona—*From Rags to Riches*

have been burned, and the people are in great distress and reproach. Reproach, according to *Webster's New World College Dictionary*, means to accuse, blame, fault, feel ashamed. These people had not lived according to the Word of God, and they were living the consequences of their actions—blaming, faulting, and carrying shame.

Distress means the inability to come up with a good standard.[8] The escaped Jews could not come up with a good standard about life. Every day they walked through the city, through the crumpled stones, and through the ashes, looking at what they had once had. They walked, looking at the temple, now empty and cold, and looking at the walls, which had once protected them, just as God did when they

---

[8] *Lexical Aids to the Old Testament, Hebrew*, #7351.

walked with Him, now in heaps around their feet.

When we were young, my daddy would burn the grass each spring to get greener grass from the new growth. When the burning had stopped and it was safe, my sisters and I would run through the yard, making trails through the black grass. When we finished, we were covered in soot from head to toe. Then we would chase anyone who tried to clean us up, threatening to rub it on them!

When the refugees were walking through the city, they got covered in the dust and soot from the destruction. Their sorrow was so great that they could not come up with a plan of restoration. So they walked around the city, wearing an inner robe of reproach and an outer robe of soot.

A New Persona—*From Rags to Riches*

I see women like this, and I'm sure you do too—women who seem to have no joy. Though they smile, there is no happiness in their eyes. They are wearing a robe of reproach. They beat themselves up, they feel insecure, and despite their best efforts, they cannot come up with a good standard to change their situation.

After my divorce, I wore a robe of reproach for a long time. Undeserved guilt, guilt that I *did* deserve, depression, and shame—all of these were threads in my apparel. When a woman has the stigma of reproach on her, it is very difficult to come out from under it. Just as the story in the book of Nehemiah, when the children of Israel began to return to and rebuild Jerusalem, which had been burned and destroyed by King Nebuchadnezzar, they met with resistance from the enemies of Judah and Israel. They met with those who tried to keep them from rebuilding the ruins. Their enemies did not want the children of God to be all that He had created them to be. The enemies of Israel did not want Israel to be restored. They did not want Israel to become a productive, healthy people. The enemies of Israel wanted them to stay in the devastation. According to Matthew Henry's Commentary, these enemies were envious of Israel.[9] They had made fun of Israel, but now Israel was being honored by the support of the King. Change is not easy for some, especially when they are not the ones benefiting. The fact that we are changing means they must change, too. They have to think differently about us and talk differently to us,

---

[9] Henry, *Commentary, Nehemiah*, 493.

A New Persona—*From Rags to Riches*

and the hardest part is that our change causes them to look inside themselves and make an evaluation. But most people don't like change, so they resist it in themselves and in us.

The children of Israel were changing. They were becoming a people of God again. They were taking the ashes and burned buildings and rebuilding them. Because of this change they would not be a people without a means and without a place to call home. They would no longer be a people of contempt or reproach.

Now Israel was becoming a people of respect, and a people of God once again, and their enemy had nothing ugly to gossip about concerning them. Now the enemy was forced to change what they were saying. They were put in a position of changing the way they viewed the children of Israel, and the enemy was not happy about it!

Changing our robe of reproach requires us to pull away from the mainstream of social activity and sanctify ourselves. The *Homan Illustrated Bible Dictionary* says that sanctifying is "the process of being made holy resulting in a changed life-style for the believer." [10]

After my divorce I realized that I did not have a good standard by which to measure my life. Praying to Christ for help, I asked Him to choose a husband for me if that was His will for my life.

Then I stopped dating for one year.

---

[10] *Holman Illustrated Bible Dictionary*, Holman Bible Publishers (Nashville, TN 2003), 1443.

A New Persona—*From Rags to Riches*

I did not even let anyone introduce me to new people. I spent that time with the Lord, reading His Word, practicing believing Him, and allowing Him to sanctify me.

At the end of that year, I emerged knowing more about who I was created to be and to whom I truly belonged. It was not long afterwards that I met my husband.

During that year I began to exchange my robe of reproach for a robe of righteousness—not righteousness of my own making, but His righteousness. The robe of reproach was made of lead, but the robe of righteousness was made of purest linen, and He declared it "without wrinkle or blemish."

Thank you, Lord.

Thank you.

String of Pearls

Wearing our new persona that is without spot or wrinkle before the world, wearing what Christ has provided for me, is a joy that I enjoy sharing with others.

Removing the reproach began with on-the-floor, snot-blowing, swollen-eyed, river-of-tears repentance. For me, that did not all come with one session. It took the whole year and then some. Little-by-little, the tattered, dirty robe began to come off as I confessed it to Christ, and He was with me, throwing it out as soon as I let it go. He was replacing it with a clean robe, white as snow, washed by the blood of the Lamb.

Repenting before the Lord is now a regular process for me.

A New Persona—*From Rags to Riches*

We are such a treasure to Christ. He views us as His bride. Listen to this, and take it to heart. He is in love with us! Let me draw some lines from the Book of the Song of Solomon and arrange them into a love letter to us from Christ. I will not mark each verse; just allow this to be a note to us from the Lover of our souls.

> *Arise My darling, My beautiful one,*
> *and come away with Me.*
>
> *You are Mine,*
> *and I am yours,*
> *and My desire is for you.*
> *You are beautiful, My darling one.*
>
> *Your eyes,*
> *your hair,*
> *your teeth,*
> *your mouth,*
> *your neck,*

String of Pearls

your form
—they are all perfect.

Come with Me, my bride,
and journey with Me.

You make My heart beat faster.
The words you speak
are like honey to Me.

You are like a garden to Me.
Your fragrance catches My attention.
You are My dove,
My perfect one.
I know times have been difficult for you.

Rest in Me as long as you need to.

Then, when you are ready,
we will leave the wilderness together,
and you can lean on My arm.

A New Persona—*From Rags to Riches*

> *I will wear you on My arm like a seal;*
> *you are a seal over My heart.*
>
> *I am jealous for all of you.*
>
> *Like a fire,*
> *My heart burns for you.*
> *I am yours,*
> *and you are Mine.*
> *I love you. Christ.*

Now, I ask you, is that a man who would allow his woman to wear rags? No way! That's a man who would say, "I have something better for you."

And He does.

When Christ went back to the Father to prepare a place for us, He left the Holy Spirit to comfort and encourage us until His return.

String of Pearls

Look at 2 Corinthians 5:5: "Now He who has prepared us for this very thing is God, who also has given us the Spirit as a guarantee." Some say *pledge* or *down payment* instead of *guarantee*. The word in Greek is *Arrabon*. This word adopted by the Greeks, Romans and Egyptians from the Phoenicians means earnest money, pledge—something which stands for a part of the price and paid beforehand to confirm the bargain.[11]

Does that not sound like an engagement ring?

When a man claims his woman for marriage and begins making plans for her and with her, doesn't he give her an engagement ring to mark

---

[11] Metzger, Bruce, *Lexical Aids for Students of New Testament Greek*, Baker Academic; 3rd edition (August 1, 1998).

A New Persona—*From Rags to Riches*

her as his forever? Yes, he does! Each morning, she wakes up and remembers. She is wearing his ring. She is his beloved, and he is hers.

We are Christ's bride, the ones He loves and the ones He laid down His life to get. He paid the price for us and gave the Holy Spirit to mark us as His until He returns for us. Revelation 19:7 says, "Let us rejoice and be glad and give to the glory to Him, for the marriage of the Lamb has come and His bride has made herself ready. And it was given to her to clothe herself in fine linen, bright and clean." And Revelation 19:13 tells us, "And He is clothed with a robe dipped in blood; and his name is called The Word of God."

Our beloved is wearing red so that we can wear white. He takes on our punishment when we are the guilty ones; He lays down His life so that we can live. There is no greater love than Christ's love for us, His bride.

So we have been given an engagement ring, the Holy Spirit, and we have been robed in white Linen.

What else does a bride wear? A veil.

It is believed by some that this tradition began with Rebecca and Isaac. When Rebecca first saw Isaac, in a field, she veiled herself before she was presented to him. A bride wears a veil to the altar. When the husband lifts his bride's veil, there is no separation between them; they see each other face to face.

A veil separates us. We are separated from God, but the Son came to redeem us. Remember, when Christ was crucified, the veil in the temple was ripped in half to show that we

A New Persona—*From Rags to Riches*

are no longer separated from God's presence. Soon we will see Him face to face.

I want to show you some of the prophecy that points to God's plan for Jesus to come and rescue his bride.

> *Sin came into the world in the Garden*
> *Jesus set his face to the cross in the Garden*

> *The perishable was attempted to cover sin (sewing leaves together to try and cover themselves)*
> *The first blood sacrifice was made to cover sin (The Lord made garments of skin to cover them)*

> *Scorpions and snakes (poison of the world) began to infest the people*
> *Moses had a snake nailed to a pole for the healing of the people (our sins were nailed to the cross)*

String of Pearls

Women were treated like property
Women were part of His ministry

Thorns and thistles grew for man
He wore a crown of thorns to the cross

Woman listened to the snake
Woman was the first to listen to Christ after
 His resurrection

Woman brought sin into the world
Woman was the first to bring the good news
 to the world

Sorrow and pain with childbirth
Blood, water, and spirit present on the cross
 (explained further)

Women were associated with sin
Jesus calls the church "her," his bride

A New Persona—*From Rags to Riches*

What other associations can you find?

From the beginning of time, our Bridegroom has had a plan to redeem us. In the Garden of Eden, and all through the Old Testament, we see examples of what Christ would do and what He would be like. Isaiah tells us that He was a man of sorrow. He experienced all the sorrows we would ever know and yet did not give into the desires of this world. Even women's sorrows of childbearing and the mental and emotional sorrow and pain of bringing up a child were addressed on the cross. Look at the following verse.

1 John 5:6-8 tells us, "This is He who came by water and blood—Jesus Christ; not only by water, but by water and blood. And it is the Spirit who bears witness, because the Spirit is

truth. *For there are three that bear witness in heaven* (to Jesus Christ) *the Spirit and the water and the blood;* and these three are in agreement." (italics added for emphases)

On earth the three that agree and bear witness to the Father concerning the Son are spirit, water, and blood. The spirit is not the Holy Spirit; it is the spirit in us that belongs to God, the spirit that will return to God and that hears the voice of God. It is what the Holy Spirit influences in us. It is our connection to God. It is the thing of value that Christ came to save.

The water is the washing of the Word. It is the cleansing of our soul, taking it from a sinful nature to a Christ-like nature. When Jesus was on the cross, His side was pierced, and from

A New Persona—*From Rags to Riches*

His belly came water. I suggest it was symbolic of the rivers of living waters.

Please slow down your reading, and make sure you are seeing all of this. The blood was present at the cross from His pain and torture. The blood was what God required for the removal of sin. In the Garden of Gethsemane, Christ was in mental and emotional torment to the point of sweating blood. He resolved to see this thing to the end, and He was beaten and bled so badly that He should have died then. He hung on the cross for hours. All the sin and suffering were placed on Him, and He cried out from the very depth of His spirit, soul, and mind to God because of His separation from the Father. I think that even more than the physical pain and suffering, the separation from the Father ultimately killed Him.

String of Pearls

On the cross we see the witnesses—blood, water, and spirit—birthing us into a new covenant with God. The Bridegroom has come and paid the price for the one who was more precious to Him than life itself.

Here is the thing I want us to grasp. The three witnesses were present at the cross—blood, water and spirit. They are also present at the birth of each new life. Jesus, through woman, continues to testify of Himself, to the world. Spirit, blood, water. . . Jesus. Spirit, blood, water . . . the cry of new life. Spirit, blood, water . . . I am here, and I bring new life. Spirit, blood water . . . you are Mine, and I am with you. Spirit, blood water . . . in you the world will see me. Spirit, blood, water . . . you are redeemed.

You are worth it to Me.

A New Persona—*From Rags to Riches*

Can you see the whole picture now? What began as rebellion against God has been redeemed and is a testimony of and for Christ. Woman helped to usher in the fall of humans on earth, and God sent the Hero, Christ, to redeem and restore. He allows us to know some of what He knows, both physical and emotional sorrow, and a testimony of Christ, our beloved Redeemer, in us. Christ goes even further and calls us not just redeemed, but His bride. He marks us as His own. He gives us fine white linen to wear that has not a spot or wrinkle on it.

Then He removes the veil from our eyes so that nothing can separate us from Him, so we can begin to see Him more clearly. By His grace, we are redeemed. By His mercy we are robed in white. By His own act of

String of Pearls

righteousness, we are marked as His own. He uses the sorrows that came with rebellion for our good and for His Glory. Each situation is covered in the Blood of the Lamb and our tears, creating something of great value; a lifetime of testimony, a string of pearls.

An engagement ring given, with the promise of more to come. A linen gown give, washed white in the blood, to replace the rags of reproach. A veil now lifted and a string of pearls worn. Yes...

CHALLENGE: So many verses in the Bible are symbolic as well as literal. They give us a mental image of a spiritual principle. What are some images you have that accessorize you,

A New Persona—*From Rags to Riches*

your wardrobe or your home? What is the item and what spiritual principle does it represent?

My Child

O little one, so thin and so small,
The very greatest gift of all.

Bound up in blankets, you first came to me,
Looking around so curiously.

Elegant and dainty, I thought you might break.
My opinion soon changed
after watching you skate.

My life was so great, so perfect and grand;
Soon all of this changed,
and not as I'd planned.

The drunks, the rages, the terrors at night.
How to escape without deprivation and fight?

Finally we made it out through the door.
How long it did take, I'll know nevermore.

Yet through it all, I felt God so near;
He held us so close as we cried and fought fear.

First we were four, then three, then two;
My precious young child, I did all that I knew.

We held on together and weathered each storm.
When our daylight came,
there was no reason to mourn.

I've told you the truth; to you I'll not lie.
Christ is close to you; he's right by your side.

I've raised you up the best I could do;
Now it's your life—what will you choose?

About the Author

Diane Woodman Bailey is a writer and photographer who uses her writing and photo-shoots as opportunities to minister to others.

She is also a retired dental hygienist, mother of two young adults, stepmother of two teens, and grandmother to two grandchildren.

She, and her husband, Joseph, reside in Montgomery, Alabama, with their dog Charlie and cat Lil Girl.